Notes for Singers

CW01215481

Notes for Singers

Chris Knowles

The Book Guild Ltd

First published in Great Britain in 2018 by
The Book Guild Ltd
9 Priory Business Park
Wistow Road, Kibworth
Leicestershire, LE8 0RX
Freephone: 0800 999 2982
www.bookguild.co.uk
Email: info@bookguild.co.uk
Twitter: @bookguild

Copyright © 2018 Chris Knowles

The right of Chris Knowles to be identified as the author of this work has been asserted by him in accordance with the Copyright, Design and Patents Act 1988.

All rights reserved. No part of this publication may be reproduced, transmitted, or stored in a retrieval system, in any form or by any means, without permission in writing from the publisher, nor be otherwise circulated in any form of binding or cover other than that in which it is published and without a similar condition being imposed on the subsequent purchaser.

Typeset in Aldine401 BT

Printed and bound in Great Britain by CPI Group (UK) Ltd, Croydon, CR0 4YY

ISBN 978 1912575 626

British Library Cataloguing in Publication Data.
A catalogue record for this book is available from the British Library.

MIX
Paper from
responsible sources
FSC® C013604
FSC
www.fsc.org

In memory of John Hauxvell (1926–1999).
Baritone and singing teacher.
Il miglior fabbro.

Contents

Introduction

This book is written primarily for amateur singers of all ages and levels of experience. However, there will definitely be points of interest for professionals in these pages too. It may encourage some to look at familiar issues from a slightly different angle or it may enable others to look at singing in a totally new light. As this book will be read in the main by singers, I am going to address the singer from the outset as 'you'.

This book does not claim to have all the answers and you should be rightly suspicious of any book that says it does. Equally, it does not offer an infallible 'method' or a set of vocal exercises guaranteeing success after six months. If only learning to sing were that simple or that quick! And it can't take the place of a trustworthy teacher either. The 'third ear' (i.e. a person, usually a teacher or a coach, whose ears are not those of the singer) is essential, as singers don't hear their voices as other people do and they can't rely on their own ears until their hearing is trained for what to listen to. My singing teacher[1] used to say that, if you think you're making a wonderful sound, you probably aren't.

So what is the purpose of this book? It aims to open your eyes, ears and mind to aspects of singing you may never have thought about before and to offer some guidelines for future development. Many amateur singers have never had singing lessons and never think about how (or why) they sing until their voice lets them down. Then there is a mad scramble to put right in five minutes the habits which have taken decades to take root. Golfers have lessons from the pro at the outset and continue to take refresher lessons to improve their game for as long as they play. But because singing is a natural activity, certainly more natural than golf, singers assume they don't need help.

This book is also designed to dispel the many myths and half-truths which have grown up around singing. Sadly, these are often bandied about by well-meaning warm-up coaches, animateurs, conductors and teachers. I hear so much misinformation, particularly about breathing, spread in good faith and with the best of intentions, but which can throw the delicate vocal machine completely out of balance. This may result in severe vocal distortions which can take many hours to unravel and correct.

In short, what I hope this book will do is make you,

---

1 John Hauxvell. This book could not have been written without his teaching. I also want to place on record the lasting influence of my first singing teacher, Julian Smith, who was inspirational in so many ways.

the singer, *think* about singing in new and exciting ways, encourage you to look for a reliable singing teacher (and equip you with the tools for recognising one), and increase to the full your enjoyment of making music in song.

Chris Knowles
May 2018
Ely

1

What is a Voice?

I see a voice, says Bottom in *A Midsummer Night's Dream*, but the trouble is that we can't! We don't have X-ray eyes. So, what is a voice?

I often ask singers this question and rarely get a satisfactory answer. It is obviously important for you to have a basic idea of how your voice works in order to improve it, but because it is a part of you, and a part which you can't see, you may never have thought about it or have only a hazy idea about what happens when you sing. In my experience, a basic knowledge is all you need, but I do recognise that there are some teachers whose main thrust is a much more detailed knowledge of how a voice works.

There are three elements to the voice, just as there are to any instrument:

1. Sound is vibration. First, there has to be something which causes vibration. In the case of instruments,

it's the violin bow, the drumstick or the breath of the wind-player, and in the case of the singer it's breath from the lungs.

2. Secondly, there has to be something which is set in motion (caused to vibrate) by the first element: the string of the violin, the skin of the drum, the reed of the wind instrument or the vocal chords of the singer. The vocal chords, also known as the vocal folds, are located in the larynx (or voice box) in the neck. The larynx, a housing made up of many pairs of muscles, is more obviously visible in men because of their so-called Adam's apple.

3. The third element is a space or housing within which the vibrating sound resonates or re-sounds – that is, becomes reinforced so that, from its weak raw state, it becomes audible and recognisable as sound. The violin has a body, the drum has a drum, the wind instrument has a tube and the singer has a mouth cavity and a head (hence the term 'head voice').

So, the three elements for singing are (from bottom to top): air, chords and resonating spaces.

The basic process is this. Air travels up your windpipe from your lungs and meets your vocal chords. Whether the air moves the chords or whether the chords vibrate first, causing the air to vibrate in turn, is a nice question. Fortunately for singers the difference is really not that important, because what does matter is that an electrochemical message is sent from your brain to your vocal chords in the split second before sound is created to tell your chords that you are about to sing (rather than speak or shout or cry). The onset of singing sound is a question of mode. We flick one mental switch to speak and another to sing, while using the same body parts. Singing is an act of will. Once air has passed through the vibrating chords, it ceases to be an air column and becomes a sound column. As such, it is weak and unattractive. It needs a resonator or loudspeaker to amplify and enhance it. You have two main resonating chambers or resonating media: the mouth and the head. 'Opera singers have resonating spaces where their brains should be,' runs the old joke, but I doubt that there is any scientific basis for it. I know people talk about the chest voice, but sound doesn't travel backwards or below its source. What a singer feels in their chest on lower notes is a secondary, sympathetic vibration, not a primary one.

By 'mouth', I mean the area defined by your hard palate, the roof of the mouth. Feel with your tongue from the back of your top front teeth to the bump which is the hard-soft palate join. Your attention should be focused lower than the roof of your mouth. Try singing a vowel in the lower middle part of your range, on a note which is comfortable; visualise the inside of your mouth and then *mentally* direct the sound in turn to the hard palate, the soft palate, the bottom of the mouth and anywhere else you like in the mouth. Listen to the differences in sound quality. And you can achieve those differences just by thought.

By 'head' (which is an even bigger place than the mouth), I am talking about the area, just above the soft-hard palate join, which is roughly between and on a level with your ears, and further back and up. In other words, the singer's mental focus for the head voice is not forwards, but backwards. There is still a lot of nonsense talked about 'forward' singing or singing 'in the mask'. If you direct the sound there or, worse, 'put' or 'place' it there, it lacks both freedom and natural beauty. You may feel vibrations across the front of your face when you sing a high note correctly, but that too is a secondary or sympathetic vibration. The old adage 'When in doubt, put it down the snout', i.e. sing through your nose, is also complete and utter nonsense.

It is also important to be able to visualise what the chords are doing during singing. When you sing a low note, your chords are relatively slack, the gap between them is relatively large, they are relatively thick and they vibrate relatively slowly. When you sing a high note, the chords tauten and lengthen, the gap between them narrows, they grow thinner and they vibrate much faster. For the most part they react in the same way as a stringed instrument, except that the strings on an instrument shorten as the pitch rises. There are now many videos on YouTube which show the chords working during singing and they are certainly worth a look.

Unlike the instrumentalist, you have no direct access to any of these component parts, because they are internal to your body and you can't see or touch them. Similarly, you have no direct control over them by physical means. Any direct attempt to regulate the vocal mechanism physically would be far too clumsy and, with so many muscles to co-ordinate, would result in mental breakdown. Be very wary of instructions to keep the soft palate raised at all times, because that is far too crude for such a delicate mechanism. Therefore, although we can describe with reasonable scientific accuracy what happens when we sing, we have to rely on images to influence what happens in order to sing more efficiently.

Imagery is the stock-in-trade of the singing teacher and images work in an almost magical way! It still amazes me when I suggest an image to a pupil and I hear a result (not always the first time). The power of words and the power of the imagination are extraordinary. Not every image I suggest will work for each and every pupil and so the art is in finding the ones which fire the imagination of the individual singer. The important thing is that the singer is aware of why a particular image is appropriate, as the image should always relate to what is happening (or should be happening) when a singer sings (as explained above).

Although you don't have X-ray eyes, with guidance you can train your inward eye to visualise what happens when you sing, to the extent of visualising your tones. The process of visualising is like going into a darkened room. You go through the door and bump into a chair; you go out again. Next time you go in, you remember where the chair is and you move further into the room and discover the settee; then you go out again. Next time you go in, you know where the chair is and how its position relates to the settee, and you then find the mantelpiece. Eventually you map out in your mind the whole room plan of your voice, so that you know where to find each item of vocal furniture and how each one relates to the others. The path that you take is what I refer to in Chapter 3 as the sound column. In this way, most truly great singers have been able to visualise the notes before they sing them and, in so doing, create them just by thought. I know that this sounds really wacky, but the extraordinary thing is that it works!

These are the very basic mechanics of singing. But just as playing an instrument is much more complex and subtle than its components, so singing is much more than the sum of its parts.

2

To Breathe or Not to Breathe?

Singers often tell me at the beginning of their first lesson that they need help with breathing. They usually say that they run out of breath even in short phrases and that they also need help with breathing specifically in order to sing higher notes, perhaps ones they could reach once but which seem beyond them now. They also often talk about their diaphragm; usually about how they need to use it more efficiently. Perhaps you recognise the profile?

Where do I start? There is so much misinformation in those statements. The assumption is that, because a singer runs out of breath or out of notes, the cause and the solution are to do with breathing. In nine cases out of ten, that simply isn't true. Breathing is important in singing, but it's not the most important thing by any means. Singers talk about breath support without fully realising that breathing plays a supporting role *only*. It is not the main role. Singing develops breathing, not breathing singing.[2] Similarly, singers have only a vague idea about where the diaphragm is, let alone what it does. Men in particular often point to their stomach when asked where their diaphragm is. Singers have heard about breathing deeply, but they engage muscles so far down the body as to miss the breathing apparatus altogether. They have seen professional singers make all sorts of physical efforts and assume that that is the way to do it. But it isn't. Just because a singer has a great voice doesn't mean that they use it well.

Singing breathing is a simple, natural process, but it has been made far more complicated and mysterious than it is or needs to be. That having been said, it is true that you will get as many views on the subject and as many images of the process as there are singers. Reading what great singers past and present have to say on the subject leaves you no better off, because each one thinks of breathing in a different way, even though they all agree on its importance. And yet they are probably breathing in very similar ways, just using different terms and metaphors to describe it. Singers are not always the best judges or analysts of their own technique!

What happens when you breathe? When you take a breath in through your mouth or your nose, air travels down your windpipe to your lungs. It might help to imagine a tube going down to two balloons. As air fills the lungs, the diaphragm, which is a wall of muscle designed to separate your wind chamber from your guts

2 As stated by Caruso's teacher and doctor.

(you don't want to get those compartments mixed up!), descends to create greater space for the lungs as they expand. It looks like an upturned pudding basin which then flattens and widens. The diaphragm is attached on either side to the ribcage and the ribcage expands too, again to create more space for the lungs as they inflate. The lungs extend from the bottom of your ribs to the top. When you fill them up completely (and you rarely have to), the ribcage expands in its entirety, from your lower ribs to above your breastbone. Where is deep breathing now? As you breathe out, the ribcage and the diaphragm return to their positions of rest, because 'nature abhors a vacuum'.

These movements are perfectly synchronised and co-ordinated by nature and you don't think about them during normal breathing. But there is no great mystery about singing breathing; exactly the same physical movements take place. The only difference is that singers need to keep their ribcage expanded and their diaphragm flattened for as long as possible to delay extra pressure on the lungs. And that can be done with imagination and practice. Imagine a series of rubber bands extending from the ribcage to the front, back and sides. The rubber bands counteract the natural tendency of the ribcage and diaphragm to return to their positions of rest. No squeezing involved, no chest-puffing, no buttock-clenching. Try to keep your ribcage expanded and your posture open, even when the lungs are deflating and you feel like caving in. And by 'try', I mean will it to happen.

Here are some practical tips and observations:

1. In general, get into the habit of breathing/taking air in through *the mouth*, not through the nose (except perhaps in certain breathing exercises, but even so you run the risk of setting up an unhelpful habit for the real thing). Why? Because in singing there is rarely time to breathe through the nose and it takes unnecessary effort. You will see singers, good ones, breathe that way, but on the whole it is better to avoid it in the early stages of training.

2. Take in the breath in the way you are going to use it. If you are about to sing a fast passage, take the breath in energetically and quickly. For a slow passage, take it in relatively slowly.

3. Only take in enough air for the phrase you are going to sing. A short phrase, say, in an exercise, does not require a lungful; and breathing on top of air you have not used ('stale' air) will cause difficulties, because you will have to expel the excess before taking the next breath in, which takes time and is uncomfortable. If you do proper swimming breathing, you will immediately recognise the symptoms! If you have to sing a series of short phrases, it may be best to take one breath to last several phrases. Sadly, singers are often encouraged to always take in the maximum amount of air. Why work harder than you need to?

4. The action of taking in air and emitting the note should be one uninterrupted, fluent cycle. Make sure that you are not taking in air and holding it, even for a fraction of a second, because the vocal mechanism needs to run as smoothly as a finely tuned engine. Holding on to breath is the equivalent of stalling. Timing is crucial in getting breathing right to synchronise with the music.

5. When you take in breath, let your mouth fall open naturally and be careful that your mouth doesn't become rigid or adopt a gripped position, as this will affect the sound you make the split second after. Rigidity of any sort anywhere in the mechanism – posture, mouth, face, shoulders, neck – will have a negative knock-on effect on the larynx and on all those muscles which regulate the vocal chords.

6. Your shoulders should not be raised or rise during the intake of breath. Just let your arms hang naturally, like buckets from a milkmaid's yoke! Let your lungs and ribcage do the work; they don't need any help from other parts of the body.

7. Don't breathe too high or too low. Remember where your lungs are: not in your stomach. Breathing too low is usually brought about because singers have misunderstood what and where the diaphragm is and so they flex/tense their stomach muscles in the

mistaken belief that they are breathing deeply. And breathing too high is like hyperventilating or panting and does not help at all.

8. Taking in breath should be like throwing a light switch – you should light up. The action of taking the breath should switch you into singing mode: a state of heightened alertness full of energy, adrenaline and electricity. Singing is not like speaking, even though it uses the same body parts. The Italians talk about *ispirare la rosa* – breathing in as though you are smelling a rose. It is a pleasurable experience which opens and engages your senses and your pores. It lifts your spirits and to some extent may affect your face and internal mouth shape, but don't dwell too much on those aspects. For instance, you may hear teachers and singers talking about smiling when they sing, because they think it has a positive effect on their singing, but the gain is a short-term one and, like so many aspects of singing, it's a half-truth. And, after all, if you are singing a sad song, you don't want to be smiling.

9. The two main problems are taking in just enough air for the phrase you have to sing and then not letting it out/using it up too quickly. Singers often take in the right amount and then let it all out on the first few notes of the phrase in a rush of air. It has to be rationed and apportioned. Think of blowing a wind instrument and forcing all the air through on the

first few notes. And sometimes singers simply do not take in enough to get them through a long phrase. However, there are very few occasions where you have to sing a really long phrase requiring a full tank of breath. Very few.

10. Be careful that you are not controlling air from the throat. It is possible to breath in at throat level (or so it feels) and constrict the throat in so doing. The air needs to flow freely from the lungs up through the vocal chords.

11. There is always more air in your lungs than you think. Try singing a phrase without taking a preliminary breath. With a little practice you will be able to get through a musical phrase of average length. It takes a steady nerve and a determination to forget the habits of a lifetime, but it's worth it.

However, in a very fundamental sense, I have put the cart before the horse, because what really regulates breathing is not your lungs, but what happens at chord level. Your vocal chords (there are actually four of them, but it is easier to visualise two) are tiny: on average half an inch long in women and three quarters of an inch in men. Men have longer chords than women because their voices are deeper (think of the length of the strings on a piano – longer at the bottom and shorter at the top). The gap between the chords when they are vibrating is also tiny. You simply don't need huge amounts of air going through them. If you have too much air, the sound becomes breathy. Singers assume that breath drives the voice and then, when the voice doesn't work, they conclude that they have breathing problems. The chords and the vocal apparatus together make up a delicate mechanism, which is easily upset by excess breath. On the whole, you really don't need much breath to sing properly. Less is always more. I repeat Point 11 above: try singing without taking a breath and you'll be surprised how long you can last.

In conclusion, I firmly believe that, if the chordal/ laryngeal adjustment is correct, the breathing will adjust naturally in support. Breathing takes a supporting or secondary role; vocal adjustment is the main part.

3

Learn to Lean

I ended the previous chapter by saying that I had put the cart before the horse by talking about breathing before chordal/laryngeal adjustment and I am now going to explain why.

Most singers get obsessed with breath, breathing and 'support', because they think that breath controls sound. I see it the other way round: the way you think about sound dictates how your breathing apparatus works. In other words, if you get the sound right (and I use the term very loosely at this stage of the argument), the breath will follow; it will support your voice without you having to think about it.

I have already explained that the breath which comes up from your lungs to your vocal chords is an air column below the vocal chords and a sound column above them. I encourage pupils to think only of the sound column, starting at the vocal chords and rising into the mouth and the head. And not only to think about it, but to see it in their mind's eye as they sing (certainly in the practice stage), as mentioned in the last chapter. Singing is always more about visualisation than about doing. Thinking about singing in this way tends to prevent excessive concentration on the lungs and on blasting air through the chords. But it emphatically does not suggest any notion of supporting from the neck.

I also explained earlier that, because you can't see directly into your vocal mechanism, you have to use your imagination, your mind's eye. Let's take a practical example. Say you want to sing an AH vowel on a G in the middle of your voice (not the top G and not the bottom). Imagine a sound column or beam coming up from your vocal chords to the middle of your hard palate. At the point of intersection, 'lay' or 'lean' the vowel (AH) as though on a small platform on the top of the beam or column, like applying a bow to a violin string, firmly and positively, or like a plane coming into a smooth landing on a runway. To offer another image, it is like laying a ball on top of a water column. The ball stays on top, buoyantly supported by the active water column. Or a balloon on top of an air jet.

I repeat that this is nothing directly physical, but merely a picture, a mental image. But it is a picture which produces a physical result. The expression 'leaning the vowel' comes from the Italian verb *appoggiare*, which means 'to lean'. The thought process of leaning is purposeful and confident, but never aggressive or violent. That is why the expression 'attack' when applied to singing is so unhelpful and misleading. When the singer gets the leaning approach right, the result is a note of beauty and power, and it will be in tune. Nature is a wonderful thing, providing you don't get in the way of it!

I am going to mention at this point something I will take up again in Chapter 9. The feeling you get when singing a particular vowel on a particular note, the sensation of singing a vowel at pitch, is a more reliable guide than the sound itself for assessing whether the technique is correct and for being able to reproduce the correct sound at will.

We tend to think of a sound wave as a wavy line, because that is what we see on an oscilloscope. However, a sound column is an eddying of sound waves; they go round and round in circles as they rise like champagne bubbles; they spin. You may have heard singers talk about the spin of the voice and this is what they are referring to. It helps to imagine a spinning sound column. This does *not* mean *making* a spin, just thinking of or imagining one. The effect when you get it right is that the voice flows, like putting oil in an engine to make it run smoothly. What you are doing is helping the chords to vibrate. This is another (and better) way of 'singing on the breath' (*cantare sul fiato*). Choral singers often baulk at the idea of vibrato, but vibrato just means 'vibrated' and you can't have sound without vibration. It's what sound is. What singers are reacting against is vibrato out of control, which is technically called tremolo and popularly known as wobble. Singers joke that tremolo produces a very friendly voice: one which waves at you uncontrollably! That is just bad singing.

I have deliberately avoided reference to 'placing the vowel' or 'placing the voice/note' because that tends to suggest a static position, whereas laying the vowel on the sound column is an expression of something active, vibrant, moving and free.

To recap: in order to sing a G, try seeing in your mind's eye a spinning sound column coming up from your vocal chords to the middle of your hard palate and lean the AH vowel on top of it. In order to sustain the sound for any length of time, you keep the sound spinning on the end of the beam – by imagination and visualisation, not direct physical manipulation. When you get this right, the breathing apparatus just falls into line and supports the voice; you don't have to think about breathing beyond taking a breath before you sing. In fact, you will be surprised how little breath you need to take in for the voice to work effortlessly.

As the notes rise, the sound column rises with them (actually, in advance of them, as far as the singer is concerned). It requires great willpower not to 'do' anything, but just to see a rising sound column with the vowel on top of it and allow the sound to happen. In effect, you are clearing yourself and your preconceptions out of the way to allow nature to work as it is intended to do. As the notes rise and the column rises with the AH on top of it, the beam moves gradually from the middle of the hard palate along the arc of the hard palate to the soft-hard palate join. In other words, it travels backwards. This runs counter to what many singers think happens, and to the picture they construct when they hear other singers sing properly. "Her voice is so wonderfully forward," singers might say. But it is an aural illusion. If the sound is directed forward, it enters a cul-de-sac and therefore goes nowhere. If the sound is directed as I have just described, it is *reflected* or *hooked* into the front of the face, having started life further back, thus gaining a further dimension of resonance.

The upward and slightly backward progression continues along the arc of the palate to the soft-hard palate join up to C#. On D, the beam goes above that join into the head. Thereafter the beam continues to lengthen, although in smaller degrees, and to shift back until the top of your range is reached. This is the area of resonation called the head voice.

The vowels are laid on (or leaned against) the top of the beam and are modified according to pitch. Consonants are also laid on top of the column. In addition, the direction of the column and the concept of the vowel at pitch (i.e. thinking AW, but singing AH) are directly related. If one is not right, the other won't be either. Vowel modification is discussed in detail in Chapter 8.

Another image which helps with the correct lengthening and correct direction of the chords starts with an internal command. As you sing up a scale or a phrase and move from one note to the next, think of a 'pull back and lift up' movement: pull back, lift up and lean the vowel on the new level. This encourages the sound column to travel backwards as it rises. Both parts of the instruction are vital. If you pull back only, the sound disappears down your throat; if you lift up only, the sound gets stuck. You can see that this is the image of a staircase going up and back from your mouth into your head, with the steps getting smaller and closer together as the notes rise. Why? Because by thinking smaller as you sing higher, you are mirroring what is happening to the vocal chords, which are thinning, lengthening and becoming tauter, and the gap between them is growing narrower.

The image of the staircase sits quite comfortably in practice with the sound column, even though they seem contradictory. They complement each other, because they are designed to achieve the same thing.

Please note that this is an enormous simplification and is designed to give you a glimpse into what singing is really about. I say again: you cannot learn how to sing from a book.

4

Slurred Singing

One of the results of singers singing en masse is they often lose their ability to maintain a true legato when singing on their own. What tends to happen is that large choirs produce a wash of sound which needs greater definition if individual notes are to be heard. The result is that choir singers overemphasise each note for the sake of clarity and lose the ability to sing phrases smoothly when they sing on their own. Or, conversely, they concentrate too much on the shape of the phrase and gloss over the detail. I regularly hear both problems in lessons.

The Italian word 'legato' means 'bound together' and when a singer sings a legato passage they are binding each note to the one before and the one after to produce a seamless sound. I've heard it called 'wall-to-wall' singing, which expresses it rather well. When singers do this correctly, they often say that it feels as though they are slurring. But (usually) they are not.

So, how does it work and where is the confusion? I have already described the idea of singing on top of a sound column. When you sing up a scale, the column lengthens and eventually tips back with each note, and the vowel rises – rides – on it. When you reach the top of the scale, the column is still connected to the bottom of the scale. There is no break, disruption or discontinuity. The resonance of the top note will not – cannot – be the same as the resonance of the bottom note, but both will sound as though they are of a piece (precisely because they are connected by the sound column).

One way to help singers achieve this is by getting them to slur from one note to the next, making sure that in their mind's eye they link the slur with the rising column, so that sound, sensation and image become one. Once the singer has become used to slurring the scale, they can start to imagine the slur without sounding it. Gradually, over time, true legato singing will be achieved. There is a danger that a singer may carry the weight of a lower note up to a higher one. Think of the difference in appearance between the bottom string on a piano (or any stringed instrument) and the top string. The bottom one is long, thick and buzzy; the top one is short, thin and more concentrated. The higher a singer sings, the narrower his/her mental picture of the sound needs to become; the weight is left behind. Stirring a pot of paint is a helpful image. On the lower notes the stick stirs from the bottom of the tin and moves a mass of paint. As the notes rise, the stick rises and apparently lengthens, and the mass of paint is left behind, which enables the stirring (vibrations) to quicken. You can see how this image fits in with what the vocal chords are doing and with the idea of spin.

The same slurring approach can be applied to musical phrases and intervals. If a singer has to sing, say, a fifth, and it is not working technically, I get them to slur from one note to the other (through the ones in between) until they are confident about where the sound column should go and how it feels, and then get them to take the slur out. They are then able to re-create the direction and the sound in the split second *before* they actually sing the note. They slur mentally, not vocally. This approach can (and should) also be applied to descending phrases. It cannot be said too often that singing is about *thinking*, not doing. I repeat: always do less to achieve more.

When a singer sings in this way, the breathing falls into place naturally and the singer rarely has to think about it, except when a phrase is particularly long and a big breath really is required by the music.

Of course, a singer has to be able to sing staccato as well as legato as occasion demands. The basic principle of the column is the same, but the way the vowel is leaned or laid on it is different. The staccato approach is like a duster flick, as opposed to a bow being applied smoothly but firmly to a string. So, the vowel is flicked across the column from side to side (not from back to front). Windscreen wipers are another helpful image. The column rises to the pitch and the vowel is flicked across the top of it, energetically and lightly.

Staccato singing can be used to good effect in

exercises, where it can help a singer find the right energy level to sing efficiently. It can also build up stamina by touching a top note and coming away again (like touch-landing, where a plane's wheels just touch the runway before it takes off again). In fast exercises it can help keep a singer on their toes by sharpening their skill in anticipating the direction and height of the column before launching the note.

Singers need to be always at least one note ahead technically. You need to prepare the way mentally for the next note. Mentally and technically you should arrive at the next note before it actually sounds, willing it in and shaping it by thought. It is a bit like plotting the path on a computer. Map it out mentally and the voice will follow; otherwise the voice is in a constant state of shock.

Legato singing is one of the main characteristics of the Bel Canto school, because it is one of the principal ways of bringing out natural beauty in the singing voice. Bel Canto is, of course, an Italian term, which means 'beautiful singing'. That does not mean, however, that the Bel Canto approach is only appropriate for singing Italian repertoire nor does it mean that everything sung in this way will sound ridiculously Italianate. Singing Wagner is sometimes thought of as the polar opposite of Bel Canto, and yet some of the greatest vocal interpreters of Wagner have been Bel Canto singers. I am thinking particularly of Birgit Nielsen, Kirsten Flagstad, Ben Heppner. True legato singing frees up the singer to express the music in whatever way they want and enables them to invest the sound with emotion in a way which never smacks of being artificial. Bel Canto is the only medium for conveying emotional truth in song.

Why is this so important for choir singers, if they are always required to over-accentuate each note of a legato phrase? Because without the ability to sing a true legato, singing declines, breathing goes and the voice runs the risk of getting out of sync or disappearing altogether. It is a vicious circle. And this is why all singers who take the gift of their voice seriously should have singing lessons: to keep the voice on track.

5

As Nature Intended

It is a sad fact that we get in the way of our voices. We hinder them physically and mentally, and we mask them by trying to make them into something they are not. The assumption underlying these remarks is that there is a natural voice hiding beneath layers of distortion. It is that natural voice which we are trying, or should be trying, to unearth.

What is the natural voice? Does it exist or is it a paradise lost? While it is certainly true that natural voices are few and far between, there is no doubt that they do exist. The natural voice, or more accurately the natural singer, is a singer whose voice functions absolutely naturally without (or with very little) training. They can sing any note in their range on any vowel at any dynamic and, within the constraints of tiredness, illness, emotional upset or physical disability, at any time of the day or night. In that respect they are children of nature.

There is an innocence, an honesty about the way they sing (as well as an irresistible fragility in their sound), because they are allowing their voice to come out as nature intended, not letting their ego get in the way. They often also have an instinctive response to music and their voice can convey it in whatever way they feel moved to express it.

I was lucky enough to stand next to such a singer every day for eight years.[3] I also taught someone briefly who was neither a professional singer nor even an amateur, but someone who wanted to see what singing was about. His voice just went up and up, quite fearlessly and without a second thought. He just sang. And it is precisely those *second* thoughts that can get in the way of the *primary* activity of singing, unless they are brought into line. Most singers are not naturals (as far as technique is concerned), but they can train their mental processes and therefore their voices, so that singing becomes *second* nature, as efficient as nature itself.

The singing teacher who really put me on the right track was John Hauxvell, a fine New Zealand baritone with an unusually wide range, who had been taught by Edgar Herbert-Caesari. As you might guess from his surname, Caesari was Italian by birth, but he spent most of his adult life in England, after training in Italy in the Bel Canto school. He wrote a number of books about singing, which, for all that they contain the essence of what singing really is, are very hard going

3 The tenor Dennis Whitehead in Salisbury Cathedral Choir.

for most people today. I knew the books a long time before I had lessons with John Hauxvell and they only started to make sense when I could hear the result of their advice in someone else. If John wanted to sing a pianissimo top Z on any vowel, he could not only tell you how to achieve it, but would also be able to demonstrate it totally convincingly. Caesari had lessons from the wonderful baritone Antonio Cotogni,[4] worked with some of the greatest singers of his day, and observed and analysed many more. For Caesari, Beniamino Gigli, his one-time fellow student, was the natural voice par excellence. He did not brush under the carpet the fact that Gigli became very mannered in his interpretation or that he often took liberties (as did many of his contemporaries) with speed and even rhythm, but his technique was second to none: completely natural. Caesari was also convinced that there was a decline in vocal standards (true) and that we would most probably never see Gigli's like again. He wrote that in 1958. I wonder what he thought of Jussi Björling, the Swedish tenor whose brilliant career ended with his death in 1960, nine years before Caesari's own.

Do such natural singers need singing lessons? Yes, they do! Why, if they are so natural? Because things always go wrong. I doubt there has ever been a singer who has not got into difficulty at some time or other, precisely because our voices are part and parcel of our

4 There is currently a recording of him aged seventy-seven singing *O casto fior* on YouTube. An object lesson in technique.

human condition and subject to our human variability: to the ups and downs of everyday life, to mood swings, varying energy levels, trauma, physical or mental illness. What is important is that every singer knows how his or her voice works, so that when things go wrong (as they will), he or she can put it right or seek help in good time.

When I started singing forty years ago, vocal problems were something you didn't talk about; they were hushed up, because they were a source of shame. Now it is as normal for a singer to go to an ear, nose and throat (ENT) specialist as it is for most people to go to the doctor or the dentist. A word of caution here. If you do need to seek specialist medical help in connection with singing, it is much better to consult a vocal specialist than a general ENT consultant, because singing is about so much more than the physical side of things and singers can get into terrible physical jams for reasons other than physical ones. The psychology of singing is a deep subject. Remember Alexander, who gave his name to the technique which is now practised worldwide in music colleges and conservatoires (see Chapter 14), and whose own vocal problems were the result of stress and postural inefficiency.

I am going to illustrate this with a powerful personal example which I hope will serve as a warning. Many years ago I started to feel my neck pressing against my collar when singing, to the extent that I needed to undo my collar when I sang. I went to my doctor, who sent me to a local ENT man who X-rayed my larynx. On the X-rays the specialist pointed out two dark shadows on either side of my larynx and he diagnosed that I had bilateral laryngoceles, which are the blowouts that brass players occasionally get through exerting excessive air pressure on their larynxes. They would have to be cut out, I was told. Of course I went into a flat spin, because part of my livelihood depended on my voice. Fortunately, my wonderful GP[5] was clear-sighted and strongly advised against an operation. He was absolutely right and I am forever grateful to him. The cause of the discomfort turned out to be referred stress, not a physical complaint at all, and, although I did not get to the bottom of the cause for many years, the symptoms eventually disappeared. This was because I thought the problems were due to incorrect breathing (!) and therefore I worked at breathing in a different, less aggressive way. I suspect that the concentration on breathing helped to calm me down and nothing more. Remember the familiar instruction to someone who is panicky or shocked: "Take a deep breath"! This was before I was taught how little breath you actually need to sing.

Nowadays a vocal specialist would be able to make the correct diagnosis very quickly, because it is now widely accepted that physical problems are often the outward manifestation of underlying factors which are non-physical. These might be psychological, psychosomatic, stress-induced or allergy-related. It is significant that the expressions we use to describe our emotional reactions are often couched in physical terms: 'stiff upper lip' to

5 Dr Frank Collings of Salisbury.

indicate suppressed emotion, 'lump in the throat' to indicate sadness, 'heart in your boots' for feeling 'down', 'kick in the teeth' to convey shock, or 'guts' to convey courage. If you are sad and have a lump in your throat, you will not be able to sing properly, and, if you are unable to cancel the performance, you subconsciously employ survival techniques which exacerbate and compound the problem (as in my case above). It is easy to see how those technical shortcuts and sticking-plaster solutions develop into a downward spiral which can result in complete vocal breakdown.

The message is clear. We need to develop strategies to clear the way for our natural voices to operate as they want to, not as we want them to.

6

Who Am I?

If you join a new choir, you will be asked, "What voice are you?" You are unlikely to be asked, "What voice do you have?" or "What is your voice?" The way the question is phrased underlines that your voice is part of your identity: you are it and it is you. It's how we used to recognise each other on the phone (before names and photos came up on the screen), and the tone of someone's voice also indicates to us how they're feeling (whether we can see them or not). Finding out what voice you really are, discovering your true vocal identity, is something which takes some singers, both professional and amateur, a long time and a lot of soul-searching. Other singers, perhaps the majority, have no second thoughts about it at all.

Let's think first about what defines voice type. It must be said from the outset that it is *not* a singer's range – or, more accurately, not a singer's range *alone* – which is the defining factor. It may help to draw a parallel with the opera world. There, singers are defined in terms of the roles they are suitable for (often known as the vocal *Fach* or pigeonhole, a term borrowed from the rather rigid German system of vocal categorising). Sopranos, for instance, may be a soubrette, lyric, spinto or dramatic, according to the timbre, cut, size and weight of the voice. However, the ranges of the vocal categories of opera singers overlap. A high mezzo will probably be able to sing top C and beyond, but that does not mean that she is a soprano. An English baritone may have a bottom extension to his voice which allows him to sing bassier notes, but it doesn't make him a bass. The high baritone may go up to top Bb, but it doesn't make him a tenor.

So what defines the voice/role type if not range alone? In the opera world it is a combination of:

1. The timbre, weight, size and cut of the voice.

2. Where the voice sounds easiest and feels most comfortable (tessitura[6]).

3. The personality of the singer.

4. Age and physique.

5. The darkness/lightness of the voice (although great

6 The Italian word *tessitura* means 'texture'. If you talk about the texture of a cake, you are talking about the overall consistency of the cake part, not the icing or the marzipan. Just so with singing. Tessitura describes the range where the voice tends to lie most comfortably rather than its extremities.

care needs to be exercised in applying this as a criterion, especially in young, heavy voices).

How do these criteria apply to the choral singer? Clearly, in a choir context, age and physique are not issues in vocal identity in the same way as they are in opera. The choral singer does not have to have the *physique du rôle*: the physical appearance which matches the role. Nor is personality important in the same way. Although vocal subdivisions like dramatic and lyric are not directly relevant, it is important to recognise whether you are soprano 1 or soprano 2 or whether you are a bass or a baritone. Heavier and/or more dramatic voices are harder to place, just as they are harder to identify, especially in young singers. In the opera world it is not at all uncommon for a dramatic soprano to be wrongly categorised as a dramatic mezzo or vice versa, as the two voices do have a considerable overlap. In the choir context, the same mistake may be made, because the darkness of a voice may be deceptive and also because the powerful top notes of a dramatic soprano may be considered unsuitable in a standard soprano line and better suited to the alto line.

Therefore, for choral singers vocal identity boils down to:

1. Timbre/vocal quality.

2. Tessitura, vocal ease.

3. Range.

It's helpful to be reminded of what the basic voice types are, as we are so used to the concept of SATB – soprano, alto, tenor, baritone/bass – that we forget (or don't know) where the terms come from. As a point of principle, I am not going to give vocal ranges for these categories, because, as I have explained, on their own and without further qualification, they can be very misleading and unhelpful.

1. A soprano is a voice which sings above (*sopra*) the others. If you are not happy being in the vocal limelight, you may be temperamentally more suited to being an alto or mezzo (but see above for cautions).

2. A mezzo-soprano is, literally, half a soprano, although I doubt that many mezzos would want to think of themselves as inferior to sopranos in any way except pitch. The term 'alto' is paradoxical to us now, because it means 'high' and yet it clearly is not the highest part. It is not the highest part in the modern context of a mixed voice choir, but it was the highest part back in the male voice choirs of the 15th century, when the tenor was the holding voice (*tenere* means 'to hold') which sang the tune.

3. The countertenor was the line which was set against (contra) the cantus firmus (the holding line or tenor part) and was either higher than the tenor (*contratenor altus*) or lower (*contratenor bassus*). Nowadays the term

'alto' (when applied to women) is used to indicate a low, often dark and rich mezzo voice to distinguish it from a higher one. It is defined not by age, but by vocal timbre.

4. I have explained the origin of the tenor en passant, but it is interesting to note that the tenor voice has evolved over the centuries from what we might think of as a short tenor, i.e. with a short full-voice range and a falsetto top (such as the tenors Rossini wrote for) to the Verdian tenor who sings high notes in full voice. You can easily imagine that this development required a sea change in technique, but we do not have time to go into that here. It is worth noting that the choral tenor is expected to be able to cope with these extremities and beyond, and not surprisingly, very few can do so with safety.

5. The baritone is the commonest of male voices. The word 'baritone' is made up of two Greek words meaning 'deep-sounding', and the baritone is another voice which has evolved in character over time, particularly in the works of the Bel Canto school, notably the operas of Rossini, Bellini, Donizetti and Verdi (yes, the Italians!). These composers tended to write for the upper part of the baritone voice (D to G), where it is at its richest, most dramatic and most impressive. Chorally the baritone sits between the tenor and the bass, though in practice excursions beyond top E are

rare; in most choral music, baritones and basses sing the same line.

6. The bass voice is the lowest voice, with Russian *oktavists* plumbing the depths to contra Bb or even G. In general, the timbre of the bass is richer and darker than the baritone's.

Notwithstanding, in a choir context it is not uncommon for singers to be assigned to the wrong line. Sopranos – perhaps those getting on in years, who can't sing as high as once they could – may be put out to grass on the alto line. They accept, because they want to remain part of a musical organisation and a social network they have enjoyed for years. And who can blame them? Light, high baritones may be put up to the tenor line, because tenors are universally in short supply. Very low altos may also be asked to swell the tenor ranks for the same reason, and vocal distortion may result.

Decisions of this sort are not necessarily the right ones in absolute terms, but they may be strategic solutions on both sides – the choir's and the singer's. Considerable care is needed on the part of the singing teacher in balancing what is best for the singer's voice, the singer's general well-being and the choir's needs. In purist terms it is clearly far from satisfactory that a bari-tenor may have to falsetto the very top tenor notes or a soprano manufacture lower notes because she can no longer reach the higher ones. But let's be practical here.

Let me sound a note of caution and one of hope.

If you are, say, a soprano of a certain age who can't reach the high notes any more, it doesn't necessarily mean that you are now an alto. You may just need some professional help with getting back on track. Unless a voice has been subjected to consistent abuse (by which I mean singing six hours a day over many years), it is unlikely to be permanently damaged, although it also has to be said that some voices are naturally stronger and more robust than others.

Let's assume for the sake of argument that you know what your voice is. In the professional world, a singer should know their own voice and should have worked out what repertoire suits them best. Unlike most amateur choral singers, professionals are in a position to accept only the repertoire which suits them. To give an extreme example, you would be unlikely to cast the wonderful Luciano Pavarotti as a first-choice evangelist in a Bach Passion or the wonderful Peter Pears as a first choice for a Verdi requiem. Each in their own lifetime and in their own *Fach* – *wunderbar*! However, in a choral society situation, it is expected that members will cope with anything and everything from Taverner to Tavener, from Monteverdi to MacMillan and beyond! For the majority of voices, this is not a particular problem. They can cope, with care. But for others, particularly heavier and more dramatic voices, it may *become* a problem. A dramatic soprano or dramatic mezzo singing Bach is not most conductors' ideal soundscape and singers may tie themselves in vocal knots in an attempt to produce a sound which the conductor wants, but which is not what their voice is about. The singer then has a choice: to sing or not to sing that particular repertoire.

My advice is:

1. Don't necessarily take what the conductor says as gospel, especially if you are uneasy about it. Your gut feeling is important. Listen to it.

2. Seek sound professional help from an experienced singing teacher.

3. If your voice is not settled (for any reason), it may be better to postpone joining a choir until it is. A hard decision, but better in the long run.

7

Managing Expectations

New pupils often ask whether they can be taught to sing as choral singers rather than soloists. They want to improve their singing, but their fear is that a 'trained voice' might stand out and not blend, though, interestingly enough, they very rarely say that their voice as it is now doesn't blend. In some ways the desire to blend is perfectly reasonable and understandable. Choirs are arguably at their best when they have a corporate sound and their particular sound becomes part of their identity; the smaller the choir, the more important blending is. But that is the root of the problem, because the uniform sound has to be made by individuals who are by definition different from each other in every respect, including their voices. Indeed, as we have already said, voice is part of identity. Therefore, the first responsibility of blending lies not with the singer, but with the audition committee and the conductor. If they are after a particular sound, then they should accept only singers who naturally produce that sound. However, many or most choirs do not have the luxury of choice, as they are usually short of singers and have to take, within reason, what they can get. That is where and why the problem arises. Therefore, what we are looking at across the spectrum is not an absolute, but rather a compromise, more of a blended whisky than a single malt!

To return to the question: can a singer be trained as a choral singer? I have yet to find a teacher who claims to do that. All a teacher can do with integrity – and by 'all', I don't imply second best; far from it – is to bring out the voice that's already there. To do otherwise, to impose a voice which is not the singer's own natural one, is an act of vocal vandalism. The teacher should be a cross between a sculptor and a picture restorer. Sculptors describe their art as revealing the form or shape which *already lies* within the stone or the wood; they are responding sensitively and creatively to something pre-existing and natural. The job of restorers, on the other hand, is to clean painstakingly and patiently until a flash of original colour appears and bit by bit to bring the painting back to the way it was when it was first painted; to its original state before it was overlaid with the accretions of age and suffered the consequences of misuse, including, perhaps, previous insensitive restoration. By analogy with both sculptors and restorers, the singing teacher's task is discovering and developing what is natural in a voice, working within its natural limitations, cleaning up and revitalising what has become tarnished or lifeless, bringing back into vibrant focus what was lost to view, and even sometimes trying to repair what is damaged.

Now what a picture restorer doesn't do is alter the original picture underneath the grime, however good or bad it is. It follows, therefore, that, if a singer's natural voice has, say, a razor-sharp edge (singers talk about the blade of a voice) which cuts through vocal and orchestral textures like a knife through butter, there is nothing that can be done about it. That's just the way that voice is, and, to put it bluntly, a choir is not the ideal place for singers of this type. Equally, singers who have soft-grained voices cannot expect their voices to be trained to cut like cheese wire, although training should bring the voice to its full potential. Softer-grained voices are usually ideal for choirs. Some voices are more beautiful than others, but a teacher cannot create beauty artificially; teachers are not hair stylists or make-up artists. In other words, singing teachers, even the best, may work magic, but ultimately they are not magicians. They can only bring out what's there, and it is important for singers to have the right expectations of singing lessons (and of books on singing) to avoid disappointment and frustration.

But, to return to the anxiety about becoming a soloist rather than a choir singer, what differentiates the two is more than the training of the voice alone. Vocal quality certainly comes into it, but fundamentally, it is a question of personality. I come across many non-pro singers who have all the vocal equipment to make a go of a career or step into the front line as amateurs, but who lack the personality to do so. And that is absolutely fine; we are all different. "I could have been a professional" never cuts it for me. Like the would-be writer who has never quite found the time to write, so the wannabe singer who has never had the right training or found the right opportunity. Conversely, I also come across professionals whose vocal qualities are limited or unimpressive, but who, by dint of personality and drive, have successful careers. Soloists, amateur or professional, are driven. They do it both because they can and because they cannot *not* do it. So part of the answer to the question is that each singer's development is self-limiting. Just because you have singing lessons doesn't mean that you will turn into Callas or Pavarotti. And even if you did, you would no longer be you and that defeats the object. Singing is not karaoke.

In practice, however, the problem is not as great as it first appears. I find that those who are concerned when they start lessons lose that concern as they develop, because the joy of finding that they can sing repertoire they never dreamed of, notes they could never reach or phrases which would have once floored them, totally outweighs their initial misgivings. Do they then have to leave their choirs because their voices stick out? I've never known it happen.

The blending phobia also tends to disappear. I have known singers, both pro and am, tie themselves in vocal knots in order to blend. What they are usually doing is suppressing and therefore distorting their natural voice, often not because it actually sticks out, but because they are *afraid* it might. Why? Because it has been drummed into them so often, usually by conductors and occasionally by fellow singers, that blending is so important that the very thought of not blending makes them feel inferior as singers. And if you feel inferior, you are very unlikely to be able to sing properly. Ask any singer who has had to work with a conductor they don't get on with. The potential for vocal compromise and even vocal damage is enormous. If you have a big voice and you can't scale it down, then a choir may not be the place for you. A similar distortion can arise over singing in tune. I want to make it crystal clear that I am not saying that tuning is not important. Clearly, it is fundamental. But, if a voice is produced properly, it will be in tune – it's as simple as that. And it follows that out-of-tune singing is usually the result of poor technique. The answer is not to screw up your face or tighten your voice or push your abdomen out, but to learn to sing properly!

I have already alluded to the fact that some voices are better suited to choral singing than others. It is not hard to recognise a voice which is naturally more suited, say, to music theatre or musicals than to oratorios or operas. Again, this can be largely explained in terms of vocal quality/timbre and personality. Different singers are naturally drawn to different kinds of music. It's the way they are made. The style of singing associated with music theatre is not easily adapted to classical repertoire – it's not impossible, but it requires a huge amount of work and dedication. The same can be said, to a lesser or greater extent, about folk singing and pop singing.

An example from personal experience may help to illustrate the point. When I ran an agency, I had the idea of combining – under one roof, so to speak – singers from the classical field and singers from music theatre. The dream was that singers from one division would be able to cross over into the other and back again at will. So I auditioned singers who thought they could do both. What happened was that classical singers sang their Mozart correctly but ramrod-straight and self-consciously, and then visibly, though not always audibly, relaxed into their Sondheim. The music-theatre singers lived their music-theatre numbers and got round them vocally, but struggled technically with the formality of arias. These are exaggerated profiles, of course, but they make the point: different singers are suited to different repertoires by dint of personality, vocal timbre and training. For those reasons, my vision turned out to be a pipe dream, but it serves as a useful example here.

Another area where singers may feel uncomfortable, even resistant at first, is the choice of music for lessons. Most teachers would agree, I think, that it is almost impossible to learn to sing properly by singing choral repertoire and only choral repertoire in lessons. Altos will know, perhaps more than any other voice part, how uninteresting their vocal line can be (though, like the viola, it is absolutely essential to the musical texture). To try to learn to sing by using the alto line from most four-part harmonies would be deadly dull and totally unproductive. The aim is that you should be able to apply what you have learnt in lessons to the music you sing in choir, but the route from the repertoire in lessons to the repertoire in choirs is seldom direct. Not all choral music, sometimes not even the tune, is written in a particularly *vocal* way. Some composers have a natural instinct for writing for the voice; others (who still write for it) just don't. That is not the same as saying that the music they write is not uplifting or inspiring or beautiful; just that it may be hard to sing it well without learning from other, vocally kinder repertoire first. This may take a singer out of their comfort zone, but that is not necessarily a bad thing.

Then there is the question of language. This book is written primarily for English-speaking singers, but it is well known and widely recognised that other nations have greater affinity with singing than we do. Italy and Wales spring immediately to mind. Why? It's partly to do with national temperament and partly to do with language. As most English speakers will find Italian easier than Welsh, let's look briefly at the Italian language to work out why singing in Italian can be more beneficial for vocal development in the early stages than singing in English.

If you listen to Italians speaking Italian in the streets of Italy, the first thing that strikes you is that nothing stands out. The flow of sound is even and gentle on the ear, even when it rises with emotion. Why? Two reasons, both to do, not surprisingly, with the basic components of language: vowels and consonants. Italian consonants are not explosive like English ones; they are *im*plosive, sounded within the mouth rather than spat out. You may be aware of an occasional S sound (depending on the region of Italy the speaker comes from), but rarely any other consonant. Why is this important? Consonants split up the vocal line; they interrupt the flow of sound. Therefore, singing in a language where that doesn't occur naturally is an advantage. As for vowels, there are no diphthongs in Italian as there are in English. Where two or more vowels come together, they are pronounced quite separately and distinctly (though not necessarily with the same emphasis or the same length); the distinctions are not blurred as they can be in English and there are no hidden vowels. Singing 'pure' vowels is another real advantage. Learning to sing in Italian is not a necessity, but it does speed up the technical process, once the language barrier is overcome. It really does repay the effort.

Not only is learning to sing in Italian useful for its own sake and for the technical development it brings, but it is also useful for singing in other languages, including English. This does not mean that you sing English like the *Just one Cornetto* advert (although it would be impressive if you could), but it does mean you will be able to sing English in a more vocal-friendly way. I will return to this point in greater depth in the next chapter.

8

The Language of Singing or English as She is Sung

I have already made some basic observations about language and this chapter explores in greater detail how language and singing interact. I am starting from the premise that vowel sounds form the ongoing legato of singing – like a sustained note on a flute or a violin or a held note on an organ. Consonants, on the other hand, interrupt the flow of the vowel sounds.

Vowels

The first sound a baby makes after it is born is a cry and a cry is a vowel sound. A baby's cry expresses need (for food, for warmth, for attention) and it also expresses feelings, gut reactions – unhappiness, insecurity, pain, delight. Therefore, our cries express needs, emotions and moods. And most obviously in the case of babies, but also evident in the case of adults, those cries are often involuntary (think of a cry of pain) and require no physical or mental preparation. They are visceral and primal. As parents know only too well, babies can cry at the top of their voice without strain and can go on forever (a naturalness which we have lost when it comes to singing!). Vowels are our mature human vehicle for expressing emotions and they are therefore of fundamental importance in singing, because singing is essentially about creating and communicating emotions, moods and atmospheres.

Traditionally in England we are taught in school that there are five vowels – A, E, I, O and U – and that is fine as far as *spelling* is concerned, although there are also hidden or secondary vowels even in writing. Y, for instance, makes the same sound as double E (EE), as in the word 'steely', which has two vowel sounds pronounced in exactly the same way but spelled differently. Conversely, two words may be spelled with the same vowel but pronounced differently, e.g. 'word' and 'sword'.

It is clear, therefore, that singing vowels and written vowels are not always the same. We use spoken language every day to communicate with each other and so we tend not to think overmuch about the sound of the words we use or how those sounds relate to what we see on the page. In speech, words just come out automatically, but, as singers, we are concerned with translating written letters into singing sounds. The *sound* of the word is what counts. The word 'right', for instance, has only one written vowel, but two sung (or indeed spoken) ones, AH and IH, because the letter I in the word 'right' is a diphthong (Greek for 'two sounds'). So we pronounce (and sing) it 'r-ah-ih-t', where the AH is the longest vowel and the IH (the resolution of the diphthong) is relatively short and slipped in at the last moment before the T. However, although 'diphthong' means 'two vowel sounds', in the word 'right' they are not distinct sounds as they would be in Italian. In English the first vowel flows into the second uninterrupted, but on the way it undergoes a subtle transition where it is neither one nor the other. Compare that with the name of the Italian radio and television network RAI (Radio Italiana). This word too consists of AH and EE (very close to IH), but the vowel sounds are quite distinct. They are not disjointed, but equally there is no in-between sound, just pure AH flowing into pure EE without a transitional sound between them. This is one reason why Italian is simpler to sing than English.

The complications don't stop there. Let's think more about the letter I in English. It can be pronounced in a variety of ways depending on the word in which it appears. The I in 'sit' is a pure vowel, an IH. The I in 'sight' is a diphthong: AH plus IH. The I in 'vile' is three sounds: AH, EE and UH. The I in 'bird' is a hybrid, an UR; a sound which might be called an honorary vowel as far as singing is concerned (there is nothing wrong with singing UR; the voice quite likes it)! IR should certainly never be ironed out to AH, because 'bird' would become 'bard' and this would change the meaning. Singers have to sound out the word to see what singing vowels it contains.

So what singing vowel sounds *do* we have in English? A lot more than five:

Vowel Group	**Example**	**Pronunciation**
OO	Boot; foot	OO/UH (long and short)
O	Boat; hope	OH(long)
O	God	Short O
AW	Bought; fort; caught; prawn	AW
EE/IH	Feet; fit	EE/IH (long and short)
EH/AY	Bet; bait	EH/AY
AH/A/UR/IR	Cart; cat; curt	AH (long), A (short), UR (like 'bird')

Please note that the English OH is not, and never can be, a pure vowel sound, but is always a diphthong: OH-OO (long OH, short OO). The pure form is O, as in the word 'God', and that is how the written O in Italian should be pronounced, even when it is very closed. AY is a special diphthong in English, along the lines of the word 'right' we analysed above: it has two sounds which run into each other, forming a hybrid sound which is characteristically English.

I have listed the vowels above in that particular order for two reasons. First, to underline the fact that singing vowels and spelling vowels are different. Secondly, because that is the order on the arc of the hard palate in which the vowels appear to the singer to resonate on their lowest note (whatever that is). On the lowest note, the arc extends from just behind the top front teeth to the middle of the hard palate, i.e. an OO vowel is the furthest forward on the lowest note and an AH is furthest back, but no further back than the middle of the hard palate.

But there are hidden vowels too. In speech, Y is sometimes sounded as a vowel, as in the word 'steely', which we have already talked about, and sometimes it appears as though it's sounded like a consonant, as in 'yard'. But if you say Y as in 'yard' really slowly, you may become aware that there is a tiny EE at the front end of the sound. If you think an EE in front of a Y when you sing it (and I mean think, not make), the sound goes into a different, and better, place than if you didn't think it. The same is true of W. In 'water', the W is preceded by an OO thought. If you think an OO in front of a W when you sing it (same caveat applies as above), the sound goes into a different, and better, place than if you didn't think it. For further discussion see Appendix 4.

To get the maximum technical advantage out of vowels (to sing better), you have to sing/think through each and every one, however short. It used to be the practice in certain musical circles to iron out diphthongs, resulting in pronunciation which was at best not English and at worst downright weird. And, unbelievably, there are still pockets of musical life where that practice persists. Or you may hear half-truths (a very common occurrence in singing at all levels). I remember an eminent conductor insisting that the way to sing 'lamb' was 'l-eh-mb' (EH as in 'lemon'). That is clearly incorrect, because the pronunciation of the word becomes distorted or sounds dated, à la 1940s BBC. But there is truth hidden in what he said, because if you *think* EH when singing that short (ugly) English A sound (as in so many English words – 'and', 'that', 'can', 'as' etc.), you get a different and more beautiful result. But the trick is singing one vowel and simultaneously thinking another. This produces changes in the tongue and soft palate, which in turn produce changes in the vocal mechanism (most importantly the larynx and chords), resulting in a slightly different, acoustically enhanced shape, i.e. it sounds more beautiful *without being distorted*.

So, in singing you have to think about language as a singer, not as a speller. And many singers find that really hard. It is nothing to do with intelligence; it is just a different way of thinking, but it is absolutely fundamental to good singing. It may well require a lot of spadework: working out the vowels and writing them into the score, word by word, syllable by syllable, sound by sound. The vocal scores of most professionals are littered with these sorts of markings, so it's not something to be ashamed of. The reverse, in fact! It shows you are being conscientious and professional and want to get it right. Eventually, singing vowels will become second nature and you will only have to work them out on rare occasions, e.g. when you are singing in a foreign language, especially for the first time. Other singers, however, manage quite easily and their vowels need only an occasional correction or fine-tuning. You will find examples to help you in the appendix.

This seems an appropriate place to talk briefly about regional accents, by which I mean regional accents within the UK in so far as they affect pronunciation. It used to be the norm that singers sang with received pronunciation, erasing all trace of their natural accent as used in speech. To a certain extent, this also took away their individuality. By and large, that thinking still predominates, but it has become more flexible, more tolerant and more encouraging of local colour. Bryn Terfel is a great example of a singer who does not suppress his Welsh identity when singing English. One example will illustrate the point. Listen to him singing *The Vagabond* (*Songs of Travel*, Vaughan Williams) and you will hear that he pronounces the word 'ask' in the phrase *All I ask, the Heavens above* with a short A. It sounds perfectly natural, unselfconscious. However, ask a choir to do that and it will sound odd and be frowned upon, unless they are singing a local song.

The complexity of vocal vowels does not stop with the basic analysis of the singing vowel sounds. The way a singer thinks about a vowel should be related to the pitch and the dynamic on/at which the vowel is sung. This is known as modification or adjustment. Singers often baulk at this idea because they fear it will sound artificial, over-trained or distorted. The reverse is true. In modifying the vowel according to pitch and dynamic, the singer is in effect creating the right *natural* acoustic shape and allowing the voice to fill it. And that is the opposite of distortion! If a vowel becomes distorted, the modification is incorrect.

To give a simplified illustration: the AH vowel you sing in the lower middle part of your voice will be, broadly speaking, the AH sound as in 'father' or 'bravo', i.e. as in speech. When you sing an AH vowel an octave above, you will need to think differently about it, otherwise it will crack or screech, or have to be forced. Depending on the exact pitch and the particular dynamic required by the music, the singer must think AW while singing AH. And each vowel is slightly different on each and every note. You can do the maths – there are a lot of permutations to memorise; both the sounds and the sensations. But please bear in mind that this is not the whole story – it is just a glimpse into a complex world which needs the guidance of a good teacher.

Therefore, it follows that the higher you sing, the less like speech singing becomes: you have to think in a different language. It is no longer a spoken language, but an acoustic language, a thought language. You cannot think of words as you would say them (as you would in the lower part of the voice), but as you would sound them. What results is actually an aural illusion. The uninformed ear thinks the sound is uniform, the same from bottom to top, but it isn't – and never can or should be. Compare the timbre of the top, middle and bottom notes of any instrument. They are audibly different in quality and tone. The voice is also an instrument and operates, in this instance, in exactly the same way as a flute, violin, piano or drum.

This acoustic necessity gives the lie to the so-called openness of the voice. Vowels are generally either open or closed (in some areas of some voice types they may even be open-closed). AH on a low note is open, while EE is closed – notice the way your internal mouth shape changes when you sing or say 'art' and 'eat'. But as you sing up the scale, that situation reverses. The AH closes down and the EE opens up. Yet, the untrained ear will hear an open AH on a top note if it is sung correctly. This is another aural illusion, and it works completely to the singer's advantage.

Consonants

If vowels are that complicated, what about consonants? A comparison between Italian and English consonants may be a helpful first step. In general, as I have already said, Italian consonants are implosive and English consonants are explosive. If you are a choral singer, you will recognise the phrase 'Spit out the consonants'. For Italians that instruction is meaningless, because you could say that Italian consonants are soft and English consonants are hard. For instance, the T sound at the end of the word 'spit' carries a long way in English (you know the machine-gun effect of T when a choir is not together at the end of a word), whereas the Italian T sound in *pietà* is sounded almost as dully as an English D and you simply can't 'spit it out'. It follows that English consonants interrupt the flow of vowel sounds more audibly and obviously than Italian consonants. And as vowels carry the emotion of a piece, the emotional intensity of English singing compared to Italian singing can be compromised by the language itself.

So, how does an English singer singing in English convey the maximum emotional intensity of the text? One way is to adopt an Italian approach to English consonants. This is a very hard idea to explain in words on the page and is much easier to illustrate by singing. It is definitely not the *Just one Cornetto* syndrome mentioned in the previous chapter. One way of looking at it is that consonants should be pitched to match the vowels they precede or follow. It is relatively easy to understand how the voiced consonants, like M or N, can be pitched, because we can hum at pitch on an M or an N (though not through the whole compass of the voice). But at least that gives an idea of the principle involved.

Another way of looking at it is to say that consonants should be internalised (the exact opposite of being spat out!). It is similar to ventriloquising, the opposite of excessive use of lips and mouth shape to enunciate text. Of course, this is unnerving for conductors. It's much easier to encourage singers to show that they're working at text by making exaggerated mouth movements, because the conductor can see the effort (rather than hear it), and because it is an easy concept for singers to get hold of. To feel comfortable looking at a choir not making that obvious physical effort, but nevertheless singing with clear diction, requires a leap of faith. Our visual sense is so much stronger than our aural sense. Singing is not about doing; it's about thinking. Do less to achieve more. It's the thought that counts.

The concept of ventriloquising when applied to singing is aimed at helping the singer use their resonance chambers – their loudspeakers, the body of their instrument – to maximum effect. As already explained, vibrational sound (i.e. what is produced by your vocal chords) has to have a space within which to resonate, re-sound or be reinforced. Our natural resonators are the mouth and the head and it is towards those spaces that our sound needs to be directed (mentally, not physically) in order to be amplified. And that applies both to vowels *and* consonants. Consonants are up there on top of the sound column with the vowels. In general, if you lay or lean the consonant on top of the sound column in the same way as the vowel, the right effect will be produced.

But it has to be said that choirs do tend to concentrate on consonants and neglect vowels. This is partly because of misinformation and partly because it's much easier for many singers to spit out a consonant than sustain a vowel. So, excessive concentration on consonants may actually be a cop-out for proper singing. If you listen to a choir in a large building, especially one with a generous acoustic like a cathedral, you will often hear a series of explosive consonants with little sound in between. It's like having the bread of a sandwich without the filling, and it leaves you feeling empty and undernourished. That's not what real singing is about.

Having made that point, I need to qualify it. Singing is performing and live performance requires a certain exaggeration. The text of a song does need to be 'put across' more strongly and more obviously than most people are used to doing in everyday speech. You might think of people reading the lessons in church; how some are clear and others mumble. But there are ways of making the text clear which go against efficient singing and other ways which allow the singer to remain 'in the singing condition or mode'.

Approaching consonants in this way definitely doesn't mean that they aren't clear or that they're fudged or sound drunk or are missed out altogether. When enunciated correctly, when sounded at pitch and integrated with the vowel, they are crisp, clear and energetic, but, like vowels, their quality changes the higher you sing. Consonants at the top of the voice are miniature: perfectly formed, perfectly audible, but not like consonants at the bottom of the range, which are much bigger. They have to become small to match the tiny resonating spaces in the head (just as vowels do). You might think that this would result in less clarity, but singers in the first half of the 20th century who sang in this way had much clearer diction than many singers of today.

In practice, this means that choral singers singing top notes correctly cannot 'spit out' the consonants in the same way as they can in speech, and they can't sustain vowels in the same way all through the range. Any attempt to do so will result in vocal tiredness and strain. If you're voiceless at the end of a rehearsal, this *may* go some way to explaining why.

It cannot be denied that a tension often exists between what a singer may be asked to do in a choir context and the good vocal habits they have learnt in singing lessons. This is an area where the singer may have to be canny and exercise their own judgement.

9

Sensational Singing

You will be aware, I'm sure, of the difference an acoustic can make. If the acoustic is dead, as in many modern theatres, or in a marquee or outdoors, singing feels like hard work and we often think we haven't sung very well. If you're singing in a bathroom or a cathedral, it is likely to feel easy and sound fabulous (or so we think). Similarly, if you have ever had to sing wearing a hat, you know that your voice sounds different and you may feel unsettled.

Although a singer will naturally adapt to each acoustic, for instance growing into a larger acoustic or scaling down to a smaller, their technical approach to these different situations should be exactly the same. Different acoustics require differences of scale, not fundamental changes of technique. What a singer relies on should not be the sound, certainly not the sound alone, but the *sensation* of singing. Significantly, one of

Caesari's books was called, rather grandiosely, *The Science and Sensations of Vocal Tone*. The sensation a note gives the singer is often more reliable than the sound the singer hears. Feeling is a surer guide to correct technique than hearing.

Many singers have a shrewd idea of what note they're singing, not because they have perfect pitch, but because they recognise the sensations produced by certain notes in their range. This is a major element of 'relative pitch' (see Chapter 17 for a more detailed discussion). A high note, for instance, will feel very different from a low one. It will resonate in the head rather than the mouth and the singer will be more aware of the upper, brighter resonances than the lower, darker ones (although they will still be there to a lesser or greater extent). But all notes produce sensations, not just high ones.

Let me explain. On the whole it is better for a singer to focus their attention on the top of the sound column. When the vowel is launched correctly on top of the column, there is a feeling of a platform, as though the vowel has landed on something tough; not hard like concrete, but taut like a drum skin, with some give. That sensation intensifies as the notes go higher, particularly on those 'lifting points' (discussed in Chapter 11). The feeling on a high note is of standing on a tiny platform, of being on a knife edge; wobble to either side and you will fall off. I think it was Gigli who, when asked by a pupil what it is like to sing a top C, took a pencil and paper and drew a tiny dot, saying, "It's like that!" Paradoxically, that is when the technique is right. And it does feel scary. That does not mean that the sound cannot be robust, because it certainly can. Once you're on that platform, you can crescendo at will within the natural volume limitations of your voice. Conversely, on lower notes, the platform is less defined; it feels less concentrated, more diffuse, while still giving the impression that the vowel could not be anywhere else. It still feels secure, though less pinpointed. These sensations reflect the nature of breath flow through the vocal chords.

Although sensation is a more reliable guide than sound, singers can, and should, listen to themselves, but in a different way from normal. Most sounds in the world are external to us and we therefore experience them at a distance. Even a noise in another part of your body – say, your tummy rumbling or your joints cracking – can be heard with a certain amount of detachment. But you listen to your voice with your ears, which are an integral part of your vocal mechanism. Therefore, unless you re-train your hearing, what you hear will be a distortion, because you are listening to your voice through all kinds of filters: skin, bone, muscle, blood, tissue. If you listen internally, not externally as we normally do, you tap into a completely different soundscape, one far less attractive, but far more helpful. You have to have a teacher to tell you when a particular tone is right and then you need to repeat it and repeatedly listen to it internally until you learn to recognise its internal sound and its sensation. This is one aspect of what it means to 'sing from within'.

When you are standing in the middle of a choir, even a small one, you probably won't be able to hear yourself sing, but you can hear yourself think and you can feel. Those are far more useful guides, but they do require a leap of faith and nerves of steel, because you must sing, listen and feel from within. That approach also links in with interpretation. You only acquire that trust and that courage after hours, weeks, years of guided practice, so that you know your voice inside out.

10

The Big Top

This chapter is about singing top notes. Many, if not most, of a singer's technical problems arise from preconceived ideas about how this is done and, in this case, from the widespread belief that high notes are the result of extreme physical exertion, particularly excessive breath pressure. Singers see many professionals putting enormous physical effort into singing top notes and assume that this is the right way to do it. Conductors observe the same thing and encourage their choirs to follow suit. Singers conclude that the approach to top notes is 'big'. When they hear a perfectly executed, robust top note, their preconceptions are so strong that they believe that the top note is the result of what they have been told to believe in: lots of breath and lots of push.

It is an old singers' wisecrack that this approach is not bel canto, but 'can/con belto'. Caesari called it 'bellow canto'. Time and again I see pupils stoking up with air in preparation for a high note and then forcing it, overblowing it or splitting it; they have to get rid of the air somehow. They ignore the fact that they often sing better when they are running out of breath. Why? The higher a singer sings, the tauter the vocal chords and the narrower the gap between them. While the pressure of the breath does increase, the volume of air doesn't. The opposite, in fact: the air stream is minute. Taking in a huge amount of air just clogs the works and prevents the delicate mechanism from working naturally (as it wants to if only we will let it). It takes real courage to sing top notes without forcing them, but the answer is, as always in singing, that less is more. Shoving lungfuls of air through the chords distorts the sound and strains the instrument. Try singing a phrase without taking a breath and you will see what I mean. There is always more air in your lungs than you think and usually more than you actually need. If you hear a singer sing any note followed by a grunt or a release of pent-up breath, you know they have misjudged it. And yet we associate that grunt with great singing!

As notes rise, the sound column rises too, but, crucially, it also narrows as it lengthens. This reflects what the chords should be doing and, at one and the same time, helps the correct laryngeal adjustments take place. As the column narrows, the concept of the vowels and the consonants diminishes proportionately, so that both become miniature. The vowels are modified according to pitch and the consonants are still perfectly audible, crisply enunciated, energetically formed (via thought) and distinguishable one from another, but not of the same scale or dimensions as they would be an octave below. Put simply, you can't sing a top note in the same way as you sing a bottom note. The approach to a big top (if you have one) is, counter-intuitively, a small thought.

This approach is also in line with the idea that the higher the note, the greater the resonance element and the smaller the chordal (vibrating) element. On lower notes the chords are relatively slack, the gap between them is relatively large and the chords are relatively thick. On high notes the situation is reversed. This goes part way to explaining another axiom of singing: that you should sing on interest, not on capital, and that applies exponentially the higher you sing. 'Barkers' use far more chord (capital) than they should or need to and will probably tire quickly; they have sacrificed resonance, probably for the sake of volume or in a fit of misguided enthusiasm. Resonance (the interest) is a singer's best friend!

With top notes, more than any others, a singer's own ears can be deceptive. When a high note is produced correctly, the singer hears a predominance of high, bright resonances, which are of themselves rather unexciting or even ugly. These 'upper partials' drown out the lower resonances to the extent that the singer may think the sound is shrill, lacking body and beauty. The sound to the singer is sometimes like fish-frying! This is where sensation is more important than sound as far as the singer is concerned. The temptation is to pile on more tone and/or volume to compensate, and distortion and ugliness result. A singer is not always the best judge of the sound he or she makes.

All singers suffer from the notion that high notes are like the north face of the Eiger: very steep, very dangerous and very scary. But where is the high and low between the roof of your mouth and the back of your head (to put it crudely)? That resonating space is two or three inches at absolute most, and hardly terrifying. True, it does require nerves of steel, but it also requires knowledge, planning and preparation. In that respect a singer is like a mountaineer: nothing is left to chance, otherwise a fall is inevitable.

I have heard many singers, most usually tenors, start to panic about singing a top Z pages before they get to it. You can hear them start to go off the rails, and, by the time they get there, their nerves are shot to pieces. Walther's prize song in *Die Meistersinger von Nürnberg* is a notoriously treacherous cliff face unless you are in total control of each and every step of the way, taking a firm vocal hold every single crevice, even if you are hanging on by your fingertips. In fact, hanging on by your fingertips vocally can have an audience on the edge of its seat; I am thinking Gigli, Callas and Björling.

The tenor colleague mentioned before, whom I sat next to for eight years, had lessons with Caesari in London and remembered him saying, "Come on, boy, come on, boy!" as he *willed* him on the ascent to a top note. It takes courage and willpower to stay on top of the column and direct it mentally without 'doing' anything. That can feel scary, but it's good scary, because you know it will work. Remember Pavarotti smiling after singing a glorious high note? That's the pleasure, satisfaction and sense of achievement the perfect ascent gives to the singer as well as to the listener.

There is also still the widely held belief that ringing top notes are focused forward. When a high note is produced correctly, a singer will often comment that they feel vibrations in the front of their face. That is natural and absolutely right. What's wrong is to assume that is where you need to aim the sound. What the singer feels in this case is a secondary or reflected resonance. If they focus the sound forwards, they arrive in a cul-de-sac of ugliness. Direct the sound column backwards and the top of the beam appears to curve forwards, producing the sensation of resonance in the front of the face.

I mentioned earlier in this chapter and elsewhere that you will hear in many singers a grunt or unattractive release of pent-up air when they leave a note, and that this is due to a technical miscalculation. It is another bad vocal habit which many have come to associate (misguidedly) with good singing. When a singer launches a vowel on top of the sound column, the image should be one of 'gliding on', as though the vowel were a plane coming into land on top of the platform of the column. When the note ends, the singer should 'lift off' the vowel, not dig in, and the column should spin for a fraction of a second before the onset and after the release of a note. Otherwise you get a dry start or an unexciting full stop rather like putting a sock in a trumpet to stop the sound. It stops dead.

When you sing a high note correctly, you will find that your body reacts in a different way from when you sing a low note. The body grows more alert, more upright; the breathing apparatus becomes more obviously involved, but these are the results of thinking in the correct way about how to sing: they are effects, not causes. Trying to turn them into causes is (again!) putting the cart a long way before the horse.

11

One Size Does Not Fit All

I can't underline too often or too strongly that you cannot learn to sing from a book and that the purpose of my writing this one is to open singers' minds to the fascinating intricacies and complexities of singing in order to stimulate them to find a singing teacher.

It is in that spirit and with that reservation that I am now going to outline, and outline *only*, some of the differences in technical approach between the basic voice types. And there will be additional differences too, depending on the quality of the voice, whether it is light or heavy, and whether it is lyric or dramatic.

I return to the fundamental image of the column. The column rises with the pitch of the notes and narrows as it lengthens. So the column of a low note is short and wide, and the column of a high note is tall and narrow. You might think of a triangle, where the base is the platform for the lowest notes and the apex the platform for the highest. The length of the column increases as the pitch rises, but it does not lengthen uniformly. On low notes, the distance between one note and the next gives the sensation of being quite big, but this distance decreases as the pitch rises. By the time the voice rises into the head, the distances are minute and the vowel appears to be balanced on a pinhead. My teacher used to describe head notes as being back-to-back or a paper's width apart, and the vowels as miniature. These images are useful for correcting most singers' tendency to stretch for top notes or to blast them out. They reflect what the vocal chords are doing. The higher the notes rise, the longer, tauter and thinner the chords become and the narrower the gap between them. It is this gap where the air column becomes a sound column and the size of the gap creates the dimensions of the column.

That much is broadly common to all voices. However, each voice type has certain points in the rising scale where an extra mental lift is necessary. For the baritone, that lift-up point occurs at A below middle C. A singer should imagine an extra heightening of the column when approaching A (or notes higher than A) from below. When they get it right, the sensation is one of sitting on a higher, more defined platform or plane. This mental lift-up can also be described as bridging. Basses have a similar lift-up, but it may be a semitone or even a tone lower. For tenors, the lift-up point occurs on the high G, when they lift into the true head zone. For sopranos, it occurs on a D, i.e. the first note in the head. For mezzos, that bridging point or extra lift-up occurs at C#. With heavier voices, the lift-up may be a semitone or even a tone lower, and for lighter voices a semitone or tone higher. Please note that this is a mental/visualised lift-up and absolutely not a directly physical manipulation.

Sopranos and mezzos have the additional colour of the so-called chest voice. The primary resonating chamber for the notes up to and including the E above middle C remains the mouth, but singers are often more conscious of the sympathetic, secondary resonance in the chest cavity, hence the term 'chest voice'. Male voices (with the exception of countertenors) don't have this particular quality/colour. Both sopranos and mezzos need to 'bridge' from E to F, i.e. imagine a slight extra lift-up to exit the chest voice and enter the upper voice (for want of another term). The lift-up is always mental, never physical.

Of all the voices, tenors have the most options. The easiest way to explain it is to talk in terms of colour. The tenor's vocal palette has more colours, especially around F and F#, in what is known as the 'passaggio' (upper D to F#). So, on an AH vowel, an F can be sung open-ish, closed-ish or closed, that is to say brightish, darkish or dark. What happens here will affect what happens above, because if this area is over-darkened, the pure head voice will be overweighted and difficult to sustain without propping it up (artificially) with tons of breath. You know this is the case when you hear a grunt or sudden expulsion of breath when a singer leaves a note

– although that grunt isn't just a tenor thing; it applies to all voices.

Countertenors used to be regarded as a special case, certainly in the UK. I suspect that this goes back to the re-emergence of countertenors after the Second World War, when there was increased demand due to the rediscovery of baroque and medieval music, and to the embracing of authentic performance. By and large the only countertenors around at the time were in cathedral choirs and their straight tone was seen as the ideal complement to authentic stringed instruments played without vibrato. Since those early days, the trend has been increasingly for countertenors to sing more like mezzos and contraltos, i.e. to be trained in the same way as their female counterparts. This has resulted in a warmer, more emotional and (arguably) freer sound than the whitened sound which once characterised altos in cathedral choirs and consorts. A particular influence here has been the wider acceptance of – indeed, preference for – countertenors on the opera stage instead of mezzos.

Male sopranos have also enjoyed something of a comeback and all the male sopranos I have ever heard sing exactly in the same technical way that female sopranos do. So, here is a case where the training of countertenors has changed over time to a technique of singing which is, to my ears, much more natural, although I know that many will disagree with me. For the listener it is ultimately a question of taste; for the teacher, or for this one at any rate, this is the technique which makes the most sense, because it is not out on a limb; it is not a special case.

In sum, although there is a lot of common technical ground between voice types, there are also important differences which a good singing teacher will respect and develop.

12

Rome Wasn't Built in a Day…

…and neither was singing.

Learning to sing is not a one-off; you never stop learning. The day you stop learning is the day you stop singing! And you can't learn to sing in five minutes; it takes time, discipline, determination and persistence.

If you are going to take singing seriously (and surely an activity you do at least once a week for most of your life should be taken seriously), then you do need to have regular singing lessons. Even professionals who are out there doing it most of the time need lessons at all stages of their careers to keep them on track, as it is so easy for bad habits to creep in and become ingrained. And, as voices change with age, reassurance is needed as much as guidance.

How do you choose a singing teacher? You need to find someone you feel comfortable working with. This is a highly individual thing, but vitally important. Your voice is uniquely personal to you and what affects it affects the rest of you. If you feel uneasy with a teacher after a few lessons, they probably aren't right for you. This is first and foremost a question of personality. Singing is an intimate business requiring great trust between pupil and teacher. If the trust isn't there, it's a waste of time. Your gut instinct may be your best guide here.

That having been said, you do need to give the teacher a chance. They may weave magic, but they are also human. They may talk what seems like mumbo jumbo, but give it time. Rome wasn't built in a day and you should be suspicious of quick fixes. Singing technique is largely a question of muscle memory, which takes time to bed in and also to uproot if bad habits have been acquired.

It helps if your teacher is able to demonstrate with their own voice the point they're trying to make. However, it is not essential and there are those who can get results by describing what they want their pupils to do (or, rather, to think). In addition, singing teachers may have limited keyboard skills. That may be annoying, but what they have to say about how to sing is much more important. Some employ accompanists in their lessons, but this obviously has a cost implication.

Singing teachers are all very different. Some will explain things simply, others at great technical length, others purely in images. It's a case of horses for courses. I was once invited to speak at a conference about voice and, in order to get a feel for the occasion, I went to the session before my own. There were half a dozen well-known singing teachers on the panel and each was invited to open the session by saying briefly what they believed in as far as singing was concerned. One talked about breathing, one went into great technical detail about laryngeal muscles, another talked about posture. And then one very experienced teacher said quite simply that her aim was to help her pupils express words in song to the best of their ability. She brought the house down. All the highfalutin technical stuff in the world is no substitute for the ultimate purpose of singing. It is easy to lose sight of what it's all about!

And for all that I say that you should take singing seriously, you should also be able to take it light-heartedly (not flippantly) and joyously. The 'joy of singing' should always be the aim. If it's torture for you, it will be torture for the audience. It is also important to have fun in lessons. That depends on the teacher and is a factor in deciding whether a teacher is right for you, but it also depends on you, the singer. Be focused and purposeful in lessons, but it is not the end of the world if you make a mistake or if things don't go according to plan. Beating yourself up about it is the worst approach. Shrug off the mistakes, pick yourself up straight away and get back in the saddle. Incidentally, warming up is what it says it is. Don't expect too much. Your first sounds of the day or in the lesson may not be great; the second ones will be better.

If you want to improve, you do need to practise. There's no getting out of it, no shortcut. To that extent, it is hard graft, which is not to say that it can't be fun.

Even ten minutes of exercising a day will make a huge difference. Get into the habit of warming up before rehearsals, so that your voice doesn't get a cold start, but always practise with as clear an idea of what you are aiming at as you can have at any one stage in your vocal development.

Some singers may find that they need the discipline of taking singing exams to make them work consistently. Others may be motivated by singing in concerts. Still others may be happy to just sing without a particular object in mind. However it pans out, practice and more practice is what's needed to make a difference. You can get so far with lessons alone, but you will get so much more out of working on your own and finding out about your own voice. It is a voyage of discovery.

My own reservation about exams is the repertoire that goes with the territory. With a new pupil, I prefer to have free rein, so that I can tailor the pieces to suit the pupil's development from week to week rather than being straitjacketed by an exam syllabus. Once a singer's technique has settled down to a large degree, exams are more viable. But that is a personal opinion.

If you are fortunate enough to find a really good singing teacher early on and one you feel you can trust, there may be no need to change. But that is not to say that you can't learn from other people. In the professional world, most singers have one teacher and then a number of coaches to help them in particular repertoires. Even if a singing teacher is a wonderful technical practitioner, they will have leanings towards certain composers, periods or pieces, and cannot be expected to be knowledgeable about everything a singer brings them. I would encourage singers to go on courses (and there are plenty of them around), because, in my experience, they always come back refreshed and re-inspired. Often, they will have heard a point I have been making for ages, but expressed in a slightly different way. Suddenly, the penny drops. Nowt wrong with that!

So, the message is: go in with the right expectations. Learning to sing takes time, a long time. Be suspicious if it doesn't!

13

Language Barriers

When I ask singers whether they can sing in foreign languages, they often say, without too much pause for thought, that they are OK in certain more common ones; the English, for instance, often cite French, because they learnt it at school. Sad to say, in most cases, they are nowhere near as competent as they think. There are three main reasons for this. First, as a nation we are not particularly good at languages, largely because for centuries we have managed very well without, thank you very much, and still do. Sadly, the cartoon of the Englishman shouting louder to make himself understood has more reality in it than amusement. Secondly, even if we are able to pronounce words in a foreign language correctly, the way the language is spoken and the way it is sung often differ. Thirdly, you may sing with correct pronunciation and a good accent, but it probably won't sound as authentic as a native speaker singing. Just think of the many high-profile singers who sing in English when it is not their first language. The number who would pass for native singers is very small indeed. Even the very best give away in tiny mannerisms or inflections that they are not English speakers. And yet we think we're better! Have you ever thought what our sung Italian sounds like to an Italian? The number of English singers who would pass for native Italians or who could sing Strauss in a convincing Viennese dialect, could be counted on one or, at most, two hands.

All I can do here is make you aware of a few of the complexities in order to encourage you to seek help elsewhere. Further examples are listed in the appendix.

French

Sung French is not the same as spoken French. Even a degree in French may not prepare you for the differences or the subtleties, and I speak from personal experience. I learnt more about spoken French through singing than I did in three years at university.

There are three sounds in French which cause English speakers particular difficulty: the U sound, as in *tu* (also as in the German Ü), the R sound, and the nasal sound as required by N and M:

1. We do not have an Ü sound in English, and English speakers default to OO unless they are constantly corrected and put in serious practice. As with all

other vowels, the Ü in singing must be shaped mentally, not physically. It is perfectly possible to sound it without excessive lip participation. It also follows the general behaviour pattern of other vowels, resonating within the mouth on lower notes and in the head on higher ones. However, because of the very narrow nature of the Ü vowel, the shape becomes less and less acoustically viable as the notes get higher and it has to be opened out with an OH base and an Ü pinch on top.

2. The R sound in spoken French is guttural. However, in song the R is rolled like an Italian RR. If you try to sing with a guttural R, the flow of sound is constantly interrupted and the voice quickly tires, which is why, certainly in classical singing, it is converted to the Italian consonant. You *may* hear classical singers use the guttural R, but it is very rare and then only for a particular effect. I will return to the difficulties of the rolled R when we come to Italian.

3. Singers, both French and non-French, have to take strategic decisions about nasals, as in the word *rien*, where the N is not hard as in the English 'rain', but approximates to an NG. It used to be the case that singers singing in French sang long vowels, left the nasals as late as possible and pronounced them as lightly as possible; they certainly did not sustain them for any length of time, because nasals tend to clog the flow of sound and divert the direction of the column

(into the nose). However, you do now hear singers dwelling on nasals for longer, mainly for effect. The danger is that they will not get the sound column back on track after it has been deflected into the nasal cavities, but this can be overcome with practice. The basic principle of the consonant following the path of the vowel remains true, which means that the higher the vowel, the lighter and quicker the nasal (and the further away from the nasal cavities).

Here are some observations on other sung sounds in French:

1. Words like *les*, *mes*, *tes*, *ses* and *des* are sung slightly more openly than they are pronounced in speech, more like the sound you hear in 'let', 'met', 'test', 'set' and 'debt'.

2. The same principle applies to *ait* and *aient*. *Il était* has a closed É followed by an open *ait* (more like È).

3. In contrast, the 'e acute' (É) is often more closed than in speech and comes very close to an EE. This also applies to *et* (and), and ER endings, like *manger*, *aimer*, *chanter*, *l'oranger* and *le danger*.

4. A Y vowel/consonant in the middle of a French word is sung more strongly than it is said, e.g. *balayer*, *essayer* or *le pays*, approximating to the English Y sound in 'year'.

5. Many French operas, oratorios and songs are settings of poetry, and French poetry behaves differently from day-to-day speech because of the metre. Here are some lines from the mezzo aria *Connais-tu le pays?* from Ambroise Thomas' opera *Mignon*:

   Où dans toute saison bûtinent les abeilles,
   Où rayonne et sourit, comme un bienfait de Dieu.

   In the first line, there are three final E sounds which need to be pronounced: *toute saison*, *bûtinent* and *abeilles*. This sound approximates to the final (unstressed) sound in the English word 'pewt*er*'. In speech you might conceivably pronounce the E in *toute*, but you would be unlikely to pronounce the one in *bûtinent* (the NT is never pronounced). Usually the 'extra' syllable is obvious, because in French scores there is often a note to go with it (unlike in Italian), but it still takes non-French speakers by surprise. However, in the second line, you *don't* pronounce the E at the end of *rayonne* and *comme*, because they are followed by a vowel (*et* and *un*) and the final E is elided with the vowel that follows.

6. The same aria has a rarity:

   C'est là! c'est là que je voudrais vivre,

   Aimer, aimer et mourir!

The first *aimer* is pronounced normally, with ER sounding like É, but the second, being followed by a vowel (*et*) is pronounced not É, but as in the English word 'air' (with a lightly rolled R). Here is another example, this time from Massenet's *Hérodiade*, where the ER of *donner* is again pronounced 'air':

Ce breuvage pourrait me donner un tel rêve.

And another from Fauré's *Automne*:

Et monter à mes yeux.

And another from *Faust*:

Toucher une fleur.

As far as I am aware, this only ever happens with an ER verb (*aimer*, *donner*), and only in song (not in recitation of poetry), but not every singer will do it. It appears to be falling out of usage and fashion, but I haven't yet found anyone who can explain it or provide a rule.

7. Another oddity is the consonant H, which is never, ever pronounced in speech. I suspect that its aspirated form in song is old-fashioned now, but you do very occasionally hear it:

Du haut en bas.
(*The Toreador's Song* from *Carmen*)

Listen to the recording by French baritone Robert Massard (b. 1925) on YouTube. His pronunciation is exemplary here, and also in the aria from *Hérodiade* cited above.

You will hear the same point of pronunciation in Chausson's *Le Colibri* sung by the legendary Gérard Souzay (1918–2004), and also by his teacher and mentor Pierre Bernac (1899–1979):

Il se hâte et vole aux sources voisines.

Both artists pronounce the H. They were the doyens of the golden age of French song and their pronunciation can usually be taken as a model. The aspiration of H is now largely a thing of the past. It is interesting to note that in English some people pronounce an H where you might not expect it and say 'haitch' rather than 'aitch'. I point it out as a curiosity, but don't advise you to use it (either in English or in French!) unless instructed to do so.

8. The OH vowel in French is slightly more closed or darker than in English. For example, *la rose* is more like an AW than an English OH.

9. Final S sounds when they indicate plurals are not generally pronounced unless elided with a following vowel, but in some common words they are, e.g. *hélas*, *lys* (as in *fleur-de-lys*) or *jadis*. In these examples the S is a pure or sharp sound, like a double S in

English, such as that in 'prowess'. But when an S is elided, it is sounded as an English Z:

Sur ton col frais et si blanc.
(Fauré's *Lydia*)

Here *frais* (fresh) is pronounced like *fraise* (strawberry), because it is followed by *et*.

The final S in *pays* is never pronounced unless elided.

10. *Coeur*, *soeur*, *fleur* and *seigneur* should be pronounced slightly more openly, *towards* an AH (but never a full AH).

11. Words spelt with 'oi', like *toi* and *envoi*, should be sung with a quick OO thought followed by an AH, with appropriate modifications at pitch.

12. I and E soften C and G. Think of the word *ceci* (pronounced like the English SS, as in 'prowess'), and G as in *géant* and *gilet* (pronounced in French as J, as in *je* [*t'aime*]).

German

German is more predictable than French, but still has its subtleties in song.

Most people will be aware that German has an

umlaut, written as two dots over a letter A, O or U. An umlaut changes the sound of the vowel over which it is placed. So, *Vater* in the plural becomes *Väter*, which approximates to 'fayter', but is different from *Vetter* (pronounced 'fetter', as in the English 'fettle'). Many will be unaware that, although German has three umlauted vowels, there are two ways of pronouncing each one, depending on the consonants which follow, rather like the way in which a double consonant in Italian slightly shortens the vowel which precedes it (think of the word 'st*a*ccato').

1. Compare the sounds in *fühlen* (to feel) and *füllen* (to fill). The umlauted vowel in the first verb is long and closed (along the lines of the English word 'fuel'); in the second it is short and open (vaguely like the English word 'full', with a hint of 'fuel'!).

2. Similarly, the polymath Goethe. Although his name is never spelt with an umlaut, it is a soundalike and is pronounced as a South Walian might say '*per*fect'. Here the vowel is long and closed, whereas in *Götter* (gods) it is short and open (vaguely like 'gutter').

3. Compare *Mädchen* (short and open, rather like '*med*ical') with *erwählt* ('air-veil-t'; long and closed, more like 'veil' but not as wide or open a sound as in English).

Here are other thoughts:

1. IE is pronounced EE (as in the word *die*), and EI is pronounced 'eye' (as in the River Rhein/Rhine). The rule is: IE = EE; EI = eye.

2. Distinguish between *der Weg* pronounced a bit like 'vague' (meaning 'a way') and *weg* pronounced 'veck' (meaning 'away').

3. ß stands for a double S, also known as a sharp S. It equates to the pure S sound in the English double S, as in 'prowess' and 'base'. Think of the composer Strauß. A single S at the beginning or in the middle of a word (when followed by a vowel) is pronounced Z in English, along the lines of the first S in the English word 'business'. Examples: *Leise* and *Sauerkraut*.

4. Z is pronounced TS. Example: *Ersatz*.

5. Y is pronounced like Ü. *Cypressen* is pronounced 'Tsüpressen'.

6. 'ST' and 'SP' at the beginning of a word are pronounced 'SHT' and 'SHP'.

7. W is pronounced as V; V like F. *Wie* is pronounced 'vee', and *Vieh* 'fee'!

8. A final D is pronounced T. Example: *Elend*.

9. EU is pronounced 'oi' (as in 'foil' or 'boy'). Example: *Feuer*.

10. In older texts, TH may be used instead of T. Example: *Thränen/Tränen*.

11. CH approximates to the sound at the end of the Scottish word 'loch'. Sometimes this is softened to a SH. That may be a regional variation, but it can also be a conscious decision on the part of the singer in order to make the sound carry or to reduce the wear and tear on the voice, as over a long period of time, CH can take its toll.

12. German is full of feminine endings like in *Katze*, or words ending in E plus a consonant, like *sagen*. They tend to weigh the voice down, especially if you're singing Wagner for five hours. Some German singers actually change them to an È, but it is sufficient to *think* an È to brighten and lift them. The same is true of words beginning with BE or GE. Examples: *bestrahlt* and *gestrahlt*.

13. Spoken German is full of glottal stops. Glottals are not good for singing, because they cause a *coup de glotte*; a blast of air through the chords, resulting in premature tiredness and wear. A safer way of achieving pretty much the same effect is to have a tiny gap before the vowel, usually at the beginning of a word with the chords still vibrating.

14. There are two O sounds. The first is like that in our English word 'doll', hence *das Gold*. The second is a darker, more closed sound (even darker and more closed than in French), as in the word *rot*.

15. A final G is pronounced like CH. Example: *innig*.

Italian

There are two main differences between Italian and French/German/English:

1. Italian is an implosive language, not an explosive one (consonants are internalised).

2. Diphthongs – where two vowel sounds merge into one (often via a third) – do not exist.

These two characteristics combine to make Italian the ideal language of song.

However, that does not mean that it is without its idiosyncrasies. English singers are often puzzled when they see two or more vowels coming one after the other in the same word on the same note. This is very common in Italian. The first thing to sort out is where the stress of the spoken word falls. The stressed vowel will generally be sung slightly longer than the unstressed vowel, although occasionally the two syllables may be sung with equal stress. In the following line from

Cherubino's aria *Voi che sapete* from *Le Nozze di Figaro*, the stress in the word *io* ('ee-o') may be evenly divided between the two syllables or the first syllable may be lengthened, as in speech:

Voi che sapete
Mozart
s'io l'ho nel cor
S'i - o l'ho nel cor
S'i - o l'ho nel cor

That is a fairly straightforward example, but it is often far more complicated. Consider words like *miei* (see below) and *vuoi*. And if you think it's odd having that number of vowels one after the other, just think of the problems faced by non-English speakers when considering how to pronounce the word 'q*ueui*ng', let alone the consonant peculiarity of 'yacht'.

There are occasions when a word with a number of syllables, like *miei* (the plural adjectival form of 'my'), is written under one note, but sounded across two. In Handel's *Dove sei*, an aria from the opera *Rodelinda*, the line *i miei lamenti* is a case in point:

Dove sei

Handel

cru - di miei la - men - ti

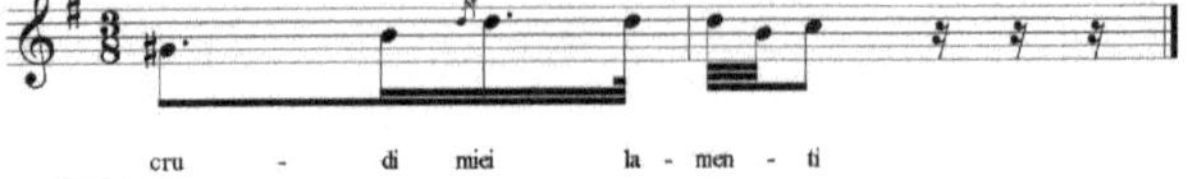
cru - di miei la - men - ti

The stress of *miei* falls on the E vowel and the first syllable is like an upbeat or grace note.

A few bars later, many singers sing the same words in a slightly different way, with the MI of *miei* falling on the note before (i.e. the A).

Dove sei

Handel

ed i cru - di miei la - men - ti

As in French, I and E soften C and G, but the way the softened consonant is pronounced is different from French. C becomes CH, as in 'cheese'; and G becomes J, as in 'jazz'. Incidentally, the title role of Mozart's *Don Giovanni* is often mispronounced by English speakers. The first I merely softens the G and is not pronounced. Therefore, 'Gio' is pronounced 'Joe' and not 'Jee-oh'. The principle is a general one: *ciel* (in Italian) is pronounced 'chell' (as in 'Cheddar'), and *gioia* 'jaw-ee-ah'.

CH in Italian is always hard like a K. The word *Che* (what) is pronounced 'kè'. SCH is pronounced SK, as in 'bruschetta' (commonly mispronounced in everyday English usage).

Double consonants in Italian are another area where non-Italians need to exercise care. Italian vowels are pure:

A = AH.
E = È or É.
I = EE.
O = O (as in 'God', though slightly darker and less open, more towards 'born').
U = OO (as in 'shoot' or 'book').

When a vowel is followed by a double consonant (as in the word 'bravissimo'), it is slightly shortened. 'Bravissimo' has two I vowels. The first approximates to the IH sound in the word 'victor'; the second, followed by a single consonant, is a normal 'EE' sound. But there is more. The S consonant is sounded on the note of the vowel 'I', something you would never do in English, even though English text on a page of music is written out exactly like that.

In the word *addio*, the A vowel is slightly shortened (vaguely like '*ad*vertisement' or '*ud*der' in English), and the first D is formed on the same note as the I and released on the next vowel, resulting in a tiny stop in the flow of sound.

Dubbio has a shorter U vowel, approximating to the U in 'pudding'. Again, the B is formed on the note of the preceding vowel and released on the note of the following vowel.

In *giammai*, the M is formed on the first note and released on the second. The lips meet to form the M, but with very little compression. The vowel is slightly shortened because of the double consonant, but not as much as in the English 'jam'. The vowel is pronounced midway between 'jar' and 'jam', or even 'jumbo'.

A rolled R is used in spoken and sung Italian, and in sung French and German. Some singers find it difficult or even impossible to roll their Rs. When you roll an R, the tip of your tongue vibrates. It's like making the sound of a pneumatic drill! What prevents the tip of the tongue vibrating freely is usually stiffness in the tongue (or possibly if you are tongue-tied). Having said that, the tip of the tongue participates naturally in forming T and D sounds, and it is but a few vibrations further to roll an R. The exercise I am going to suggest is not foolproof, but it does help some people. Concentrating on using the tip of the tongue to strike the hard palate behind the top front teeth, say, "DDD" (i.e. three Ds). Then say three Ts; then three TRs, where the R is rolled. The idea is that the tongue becomes more flexible with the D and T consonants and it is then an easier step to a rolled R. Like all things vocal, it needs time and practice.

Latin

On the whole, the Latin pronunciation taught in school is different from the 'church' pronunciation generally adopted for singing. Although as a general rule church pronunciation is more Italianate than secular pronunciation, it is also true that it may differ from one country to another. The German way of singing Latin, for instance, is different in some particulars from the French way. In England the Latin *mihi* – *fecit mihi magna* ('He has done great things *for me*') – is pronounced 'mee-hee', but in Germany it is sometimes pronounced 'mee-kee'. *Luceat*, which is usually pronounced 'loo-ché-aht', is pronounced 'loo-tsé-aht' by German speakers. The French way of pronouncing the Latin, say in the Fauré *Requiem*, is distinctively different from our English way.

The second E sound in *perpetua* is not pronounced 'pet' as we would say it in English, but 'pé'. The Italians and the Spanish would probably follow suit. These are a few examples among many. You may also find that you are asked to adopt a particular national pronunciation for a particular piece, e.g. German pronunciation for a German Mass set in Latin.

In the appendix I give a generally accepted English pronunciation of Latin, but you should be aware that you will hear variations even within English-speaking countries and that different conductors will have different preferences.

Russian

Given the complications of the Cyrillic alphabet and of the transliteration of Russian into English, I am not going to go into further detail. Suffice it to say that Russian consonants are very crisply enunciated and that, on the whole, it is a very satisfying language to sing in, providing that the singer is careful not to over-darken Russian vowels, which tend to be naturally dark anyway. Most singers love singing in Russian, once they have got over the difficulties of pronunciation.

14

Here I Stand

When you stop the wrong, the right will do itself.

(F. M. Alexander)

Frederick Alexander was an Australian actor who experienced vocal problems when auditioning for work. He watched himself in the mirror and noticed tension in his neck and restrictive movement in his head, which affected his larynx. This was the starting point of his investigation into posture and its effects on performing. Alexander eventually gave up acting to concentrate on helping others and moved to London, training teachers to apply his methods. Alexander classes are now an established part of conservatoire vocal courses to ensure physical (and therefore vocal) efficiency and well-being.

The Alexander Technique develops efficient, stress-free use of the body by eliminating its inefficiencies and strains, and allowing the body to behave as it is naturally designed to. The basic principle is not as crude as *putting* your body into a certain position or configuration, because that will not relieve the underlying tensions, but it is about relaxing the muscles (*telling* the muscles to relax), so that they are free to elongate and allow the body to adopt the position or configuration it naturally wants to. Much of what concerns singers is to do with the spinal cord and the backbone/vertebrae. After an Alexander session, singers often say that they feel taller and that they need to adjust their driving mirrors, as they are no longer squashed into the driving seat. You can imagine from that observation that the Alexander Technique frees the neck muscles (amongst others) and facilitates the free and efficient operation of the lungs, chest and ribcage.

One of the fundamental concepts of the Alexander Technique is thinking not doing, giving yourself verbal instruction rather than putting yourself in new (usually stressed) positions. The parallels with singing are obvious. Physical and mental re-education is key, breaking the old physical patterns by replacing them with new mental ones. It's all about thought process: a re-education of mind which leads to a re-alignment of body.

In spite of the title of this chapter (which, in case you didn't recognise it, is the first line of one of Tom Rakewell's arias in *The Rake's Progress* by Stravinsky, as well as being attributed to Martin Luther), posture is not just about how you stand. It covers any position taken up or any movement made by any part of the body which affects singing (which is pretty well all of them): sitting, standing, sitting down, standing up, how you move on two feet (if required to do so), the way you hold your music, where you place a music stand and how you position yourself in relation to it, how you look at the conductor. Therefore, we are thinking particularly of head and neck, face, mouth and jaw, shoulders, chest, back, pelvis, legs and feet. Posture is also affected by what glasses you choose and what clothes you wear (particularly shoes). You might say that posture is about how you hold yourself, except that the idea of holding suggests a fixed position, which is definitely not what efficient body posture is about.

Why is posture so important? I would estimate that *at least* eighty per cent of singers I see have postural problems of one sort or another. The percentage may well be much higher. And that applies just as much to professionals as to amateurs. If you play the flute and your flute has a bend or a dent or a kink in it, the air doesn't flow efficiently and the sound will be affected. And you will have to change the way you use the breath to compensate. Your body is the housing for your voice. The flute's sound column is horizontal; yours is vertical. Anything in you which is rigid, inflexible, misaligned, stressed or gripped will immediately and directly affect your sound.

Physical misalignment may seem to have nothing directly to do with the voice, but it may nevertheless have a knock-on effect. One of my pupils had severe leg and knee problems. After a successful operation, his singing was noticeably easier. This showed how much his body had been thrown out of alignment, as he overcompensated with one side of his body to avoid pain in the other. In turn, that introduced uneven posture, which affected his neck and his larynx.

But often imbalance is directly related to sound. Take the neck position as an example. Try singing any note which is comfortable for you and at the same time incline your head, first downwards so that your chin nearly touches your chest and then upwards and backwards. Hear the vast difference in sound those positions produce. Only one small segment of that large arc is right for singing. No further evidence should be needed to convince you that neck position is crucial. If you have physical difficulty in doing that experiment, please use common sense!

The neck is an obvious example. But, as illustrated by the pupil mentioned above, what we do with the rest of our body is just as important. The vocal mechanism needs to operate freely without physical hindrance. We need to train our bodies to create the right conditions for our voices to function naturally. And in general we get in the way, whether it's by manufacturing a voice that is not our own (because we think it sounds better than nature); or by throwing ourselves, sometimes literally, into producing sound or by clogging up the works with excess breath. The list is long. Our voices are delicate instruments; they need to be respected and nurtured, not abused or taken by storm. Sadly, conductors have not helped, although there is greater understanding now than there was thirty years ago. Encouragement to take in too much breath too early and to 'project' to the back (as though singers could hurl their voices like a javelin) spring to mind. And I remember that, when I started out years ago in professional singing, a standard oratorio stance was 'chin down and chest out'.

Let's consider how to stand. For most concert singing (where movement, apart from standing and sitting, is not usually required), your feet should be set apart and inclined slightly outwards (forming a V). This creates a firm base or platform on which your body rests. If you stand with feet together, you wobble. If you stand with feet too far apart, you throw your body out of alignment (and look very silly!). Next the knees. The worst thing is to stand with knees locked, i.e. pressed backwards, as that is a tensed position and one which will also throw the rest of your body out of alignment. 'Ease your knees' by allowing them to bend forward, almost (note, *almost*) as though you were sitting. This will feel strange if you're not used to it. Now the pelvis. It needs to be allowed to rotate towards the front, almost like sitting. Now *tell* your back and neck muscles to relax and imagine a cord pulling from above and elongating your spine and neck. The telling is important, as otherwise you will *put* your back into a new stressed position. It must be *allowed* to lengthen. Shoulders relaxed and your arms suspended from them like pails from a milkmaid's yoke – just hanging. Your shoulders should never be pulled back or raised. A danger point for raising them is when you breathe in. And they should never be pushed back, perhaps in an effort to 'stand up straight'. There is a very important difference between 'standing up straight', ramrod-straight, and standing to your full height in a relaxed, natural but alert and efficient stance. If all the other alignments are correct, your hands should hang by your hips. Singers talk about being grounded, and this is what it means. The aim is to allow your weight to plant you naturally on the floor.

One odd thing about getting posture right is that, paradoxically, it will feel very awkward at first and you may feel not only silly, but exposed. However, rest assured that, from the audience's perspective, you will look relaxed, natural and free.

There is one more, vitally important area for consideration: the face, and particularly the mouth, lips and jaw. Observe the faces of choral singers on the television when the camera pans along the rows, say at the Proms. Which are the ones singing most efficiently? Those who shape every syllable exaggeratedly with their lips and mouths? Those who smile fixedly? Those who look as though they're projecting, energetically, enthusiastically, bodily? It doesn't take a mind reader to guess that the answer is (probably) no! Look for the relaxed but alert face, intensely concentrated on the music (not the score), eyes focused, no grimacing or pulling of features. That's the one!

All singers, and I mean *all*, have bad physical habits which get in the way of their singing. However small or temporary these habits may be, they are sure to have a knock-on effect on vocal production. Any facial distortion, rigidity or tension will be relayed via the facial, neck and laryngeal muscles to the chords themselves and chordal adjustment will be affected. The list of potential hazards includes excessive smiling, over-exaggerated mouth shapes and lip positions (including opening far too wide and chewing the words) and a tight/stiff jaw. It can also include excessive relaxation, which may appear to contradict what I've just said. On one level singing is a muscular activity and muscles can fail to function through being too relaxed. This is where the notion of alertness comes in. Alertness or energy or adrenaline or electricity (think 'nerviness' as opposed to 'nervousness') – it all amounts to the same thing. The singer cannot afford to be without it, to be switched off. With the intake of breath, a mental switch is flicked which puts the singer in the singing mode. The singer uses the same organs as in speech, but in a different way, which requires a different, heightened energy.

As far as the mouth is concerned, there are really only two things which move *significantly*: the tongue and the soft palate. Both are involved in vowel-shaping and resonation. Any attempt to influence *directly* how these body parts adjust is too blunt a solution for such a delicate and sensitive mechanism as the voice. To say, for instance, that you must always raise the soft palate when singing is plain crude. I believe there is only one *possible* exception (and even this is not hard and fast), and that is the general lie of the tongue. If you look at singers' mouths and their tongues, you will see that no two are exactly the same in the way they change shape or in the position they assume during singing. Some arch, some lie flat, some roll back. Of course, part of the natural function of the vocal mechanism is that the tongue changes shape and position according to vowel and pitch. Stiffness in the tongue, as in any part of the vocal mechanism, is a bugbear. I was taught early on, and experience bears out the teaching, that the tip of the tongue should generally rest (i.e. without tension or undue pressure) on the back of the lower front teeth. It will still change shape. For *most* singers (though, it has to be said, not for all), this should be the default position. If the tongue rolls right back, the sound loses its focus. But it also has to be said that, if the tongue is doing funny things, the solution may lie elsewhere rather than with the tongue itself.

What of the jaw? Like all the other parts, in singing it should be free to move as nature intended. Stiffness in the jaw, like any other stiffness, is a bad thing! If you think about the hinge of the jaw, just under your ears, it is possible to release it via an 'up, round and down' motion. If a singer's jaw is very tight, direct physical intervention *may* be necessary in the first instance to free it up. How much should I open my mouth? There is no right answer, as every mouth is different. It used to be said that you should open your mouth two finger widths, but this again is crude (as well as uncomfortable – too much like the dentist's chair!). What counts in singing is the internal mouth space. The external aperture acts like the shutters on an organ, as a volume control. The louder you sing, the wider you open (though even that is a generalisation, to which there are exceptions).

This is why practising in front of a mirror is so important, especially at first, as is regular checking later on. Old habits die hard and tend to come back to haunt you unless they are held constantly in check; equally, new bad habits can and will creep in easily unless you are constantly vigilant. Clearly this is an aspect which any singing teacher worth their salt will address.

For much of the rehearsal time you will be singing sitting down. Therefore it is very important that your sitting posture allows your vocal apparatus to work freely and efficiently. If you have any physical impairment, then you must modify what I am going to say according to your condition. The ideal is for your feet to be flat on the floor (never cross your legs while singing unless required to on stage, because it twists the body), your legs vertical up to the knee joint, horizontal to the hips, bottom flat on the seat of the chair and back loosely straight. This probably means not leaning into the back of the chair, because most chairs are poorly designed ergonomically, which doesn't help. The position should suggest alertness – you should mean business.

It is not hard to see that your ability to sit (or stand) properly depends on your footwear. High heels throw your body out of alignment straight away, and also form an unstable platform. 'Sensible' shoes may be the order of the day.

The way you hold your copy should allow you to see the dots and the conductor with minimal movement between the two and, of course, allow you to breathe easily as required. Some singers use one hand, others two – whichever feels right and works for you. In rehearsal it is a good idea to have a pencil in one hand. It is possible to hold a pencil in the same hand you use to hold the score. If you're right-handed, let the spine of the copy lie in your right hand with the pencil held like a chopstick across your thumb and between your index and middle fingers, and use the left hand to turn the pages. Many singers hold the copy far too low and have to bend their necks and upper bodies to see the music.

If you use a music stand, either when sitting or standing, adjust the height and the angle of the stand to make sure you are not looking down (or awkwardly up) at the music. You need to be able to see the music and the conductor without excessive movement of the head and neck. The stand should be adjusted so that your standing posture is free and efficient.

If you are singing from memory, then allow your arms to hang freely from your shoulders and your hands to hang naturally as extensions of your arms. That doesn't mean that you can't use your hands as a means of expression (if appropriate), of course.

Many singers who wear glasses have difficulty focusing on the music and the conductor in quick succession. When you have an eye test, it is worth explaining the situation to the optician to get professional advice. Varifocals might be a solution, but please consult a specialist.

I finish this chapter by returning to the words of

Alexander quoted at the beginning: *When you stop the wrong, the right will do itself.* Few singers, even with the aid of a mirror, will be able to analyse and correct their postural problems, even if they are able to identify them. They need another pair of eyes, expert eyes, not always those of a singing teacher,[7] to help them strip away the habitual accretions of time – a bit like careening a boat to bring it back to its original condition, so that it can move through the water (music) smoothly and unhindered. You know it makes sense!

7 I am not an Alexander practitioner. I believe that I have outlined the basics accurately, but if you feel you would like to explore the technique further, you must find a qualified expert.

15

Singing Dynamics or Dynamic Singing?

When musicians refer to 'the dynamics', they are usually thinking about the symbols in the score which indicate volume levels – the louds and the softs and all the gradations in between. They are traditionally represented by abbreviations of Italian words – *ff*, *f*, *mf*, *mp*, *p* and *pp*, which stand (as you know) for fortissimo, forte, mezzo forte, mezzo piano and pianissimo. The fact that musical dynamics appear on the page in Italian gives them an unnecessary aura, a certain mystique, whereas the two Italian root words used here are ordinary, everyday words, just meaning 'strong' and 'soft'.

The word 'dynamics' comes from a Greek word meaning 'power'. Interestingly, in mechanics the word suggests motion and in sociology it suggests growth, both of which describe something which does not stand still.

If you think of someone you would call dynamic, you'll see the connection. And dynamics in a musical context are ultimately about direction, shape and movement. Music rarely, if ever, stands still.

Dynamic markings and their symbols come from the store of signposts which composers have at their disposal to place in the score to guide you, the performer, along the way towards an understanding of what they had in mind when they wrote the piece. Dynamic markings help the performer become a medium for conveying the composer's original conception as faithfully as possible to the ears and hearts of the audience. The finest interpreters will add something of themselves to their interpretation which enhances the composer's intentions and may even take the piece beyond the composer's own imagining. Their interpretation gives the listener the opportunity of hearing a familiar piece in a new way or a new piece for the first time. Music-making thus becomes an act of collaborative *re*-creation by the performer on behalf of the composer for the benefit of the audience, because for most people music does not exist unless it is made audible in performance. That is a responsibility which should never be taken lightly.

It is worth pointing out that in the case of some scores, particularly baroque and earlier, the signposts are often editorial (not original annotations by the composer). They are therefore subjective, being themselves interpretations, to be accepted, modified or rejected. Performers need to consider them carefully and take decisions about their compatibility with their own concept of the piece. Sometimes the editorial markings will have been superseded by more up-to-date research and sometimes they are just plain wrong or wacky, but mostly they reflect middle-of-the-road interpretation and are harmless.

I hope I am not doing instrumentalists a disservice if I say that they can respond quite mechanically to dynamics. If a crescendo is marked, they can *make* one via increased breath or bow pressure or, in the case of percussionists and keyboard players, by greater hammer or finger power.

But with singers, observing the dynamic is only half the story, and it is not the most significant half. All music is an expression of emotion to a lesser or greater degree and the voice is the most sensitive of instruments, as it is itself an integral part of the performer who feels the emotion. That is an advantage, but it can also be a problem. If you sing an aria of great sadness and give yourself up totally to the emotion, you may be so overwhelmed that you will be unable to sing (you will have a 'catch' or 'lump' in the throat), which defeats the object of song. The singer's duty and purpose are to convey the emotion of the music to the audience, not to overindulge in it; not to break down and become an embarrassment to audience and self. What the singer has to maintain is what might be called brinkmanship: having the ability to feel the emotion while singing, but also the self-control to stop short of being overcome by it – going to the brink, but not going over the edge.

Therefore, for singers, dynamics are best understood

as mood markings rather than volume levels and the best way to sing at the right dynamic level is not merely to 'obey' the instruction, but to ask yourself *why* the composer has marked a particular passage in the score in the way he has. What did he want to convey? Such are the restrictions of tradition and convention that surprisingly few composers expand on what they want beyond musical shorthand. Is this passage *p* because it is sad, introspective, reflective? Is that one *f* because it is angry, forceful, happy? If a singer approaches dynamics in this interpretational way rather than as a mechanical response to an instruction about volume levels, the dynamics have a purpose beyond themselves and the voice responds to the emotion. Suddenly, dynamics become a lot easier, because they have a reason to exist.

I have to admit that applying this approach to choral singing is far more difficult than to solo singing, and particularly in large choirs. But it is not impossible to think and sing emotionally and interpretationally even if your voice is one of thousands. And I have to say that singing from memory adds yet another dimension to the performance, because the whole of your concentration can be given to the music and not to all the other things singers have to think about like holding the score, turning the page and looking at their markings.

It seems appropriate to consider in this chapter a word often misunderstood by singers and conductors: projection. "I can't hear you – project your voices to the back." The word means 'to throw forward', as in the associated word 'projectile', as though by some physical exertion the singer can throw his voice forward like a javelin. How does that work with instruments other than the voice? All instruments have cases – the tube of a wind instrument, the body of a violin, the case of a piano, the drum of a drum – and they cannot project in that sense, because they are static and cannot move within themselves. You can try to throw your head back and lunge, you can strain every muscle to produce more sound, you can force your voice into a place it doesn't want to go in order to produce more *squillo* or cut or brightness, but the result is not singing but shouting or barking or noise, and hoarseness soon follows. Your casing is your mouth and head – where the voice resounds or resonates. That is where the reinforcement of the voice takes place – within – and the singer goes outside that space at his/her peril. The singer is like a transmitter: static, but sending out waves of sound.

Like an instrumentalist with a portable instrument, the singer can point himself in the direction the sound is to travel, but cannot push beyond his natural limits. Some voices are small, others big; some are penetrating, others soft-grained. You need to recognise and accept (with the help of your teacher) the nature and capability of your own voice and sing within the natural scope of your instrument. So-called projection – the carrying power of the sound – comes from the full harnessing of the resonators, not from *trying* to reach the back by forcing. It is quite common for one singer to stand next to another and think that their neighbour is hardly singing at all. But go out into the audience and it is a different story, because the sound has travelled and that is what counts. Think of dropping a pebble into a pond. The pebble causes waves which radiate a long way from a very small centre. That's the image of the singer as transmitter. Stay in the small, calm centre and never get involved with the waves. They will be there all right, but it is a question of trust.

This concept of being self-contained links in with the idea of regarding dynamics as mood markings, because singers should always sing from the inside out, allowing the emotion within to be the driving force behind external expression. The same is true with acting. This involves being in touch with the innermost feelings aroused by the music. That is easier said than done, although, as I write the word 'done', I realise that it is not the best choice of vocabulary, because singing is about thinking and feeling, not doing.

Let me offer a personal example. When I first came across the idea of singing from within, I was involved with rehearsals for a production of *Carmen* and so I thought I'd try it out. I concentrated on thinking and feeling. In the first rehearsal I put this to the test and the director asked me why I wasn't acting. I countered that I was, and he in turn pointed out that nothing was showing in my face or in my movements. In other words, I had internalised so much that nothing was registering to the audience. That's one extreme. The other is the case of cod acting, of the singer who puts on an act (the expression suggests something external which is put on like a coat), who play-acts emotion rather than letting it emerge to inform the performance. It is perhaps easier to spot that approach in (poor) amateur dramatics. Living the music or the role is a good way of describing the balance between these two extremes. If you have two actors on stage at the same time, one who lives the role and the other who 'acts', you can spot the fake a mile off. To get it right requires guidance, practice and courage.

Singers, particularly those in choirs, are often asked to 'phrase', which usually involves a crescendo and a decrescendo – what is generally known as a pair of hairpins! And that approach is appropriate to a lot of music. What happens quite often is that the shape of the phrase is achieved, but the detail of it is lost. Some notes may not be really sung, but glided or glossed over, sacrificed to shape. Over-phrasing leads to under-singing. However, it is perfectly possible to shape and not lose detail, though it may feel counter-intuitive for those who have had hairpins drummed into them (to mix metaphors). Singing is very rarely static; one note usually travels to the next. You should always be forward-looking as a singer, thinking ahead and preparing the way for the next note. Once you've stepped onto the ice, you need to keep going with the natural momentum of the music and not dig your heels or your toes in. Go with the flow! After all, it's no use looking back. Once a sound has been emitted, you can't haul it back in. You just need to keep going.

That also underlines a difference between amateurs and professionals. Amateur singers who make mistakes (and all singers at every level do) often stop, unable to carry on. Professionals acquire the knack of carrying on regardless, sometimes even singing gibberish for a few bars until they get back on track or, having made a false start, waiting for the right entry or ignoring one wrong note or glitch. I find this in singing lessons. We work on a piece or a passage and, when we come to put it together, a singer will stop if they go wrong instead of living in the moment and carrying on. Is it because they feel able to stop when they're singing in a choir because they know that others will keep going? Those who sing day in, day out soon realise that for much of the time they are not on top form, even during performances. Sometimes they make mistakes, sometimes their voices won't work quite as they want, sometimes their concentration is less than a hundred per cent. But they get used to it and carry on.

A word about volume in general. I often find that singers think they're singing loudly when in fact they're not. In many cases they are singing so quietly that their voices are not really functioning properly. It's a bit like not having enough petrol running through an engine. If there's not enough, it will stall. I suspect this is to do with singing en masse. Singers are terribly afraid of sticking out and often the result is that they try to sing so unobtrusively that they are not really singing at all. Singers need to become aware of the minimum energy and/or volume level that drives their voice and not be afraid to harness it.

There is an additional factor that needs to be considered when talking about dynamics and it is linked to all the other aspects mentioned above, particularly my early *Carmen* experience. You might call it *enhancement.* This means the heightening of expression to a level where the expression registers with an audience. That is something which many singers find very difficult, because it is primarily a question of personality. Extroverts will find it easier than introverts. However, that does not mean that an introvert cannot acquire the technique. Just for the duration of the act of re-creation, the singer needs to be larger than life, to be able to bring to the surface the feelings that may be lying deep down and which are the lifeblood of performing arts. It is the art of exaggerating what is already there. That does not mean exaggerating to the point of caricature (unless the piece demands caricature). As with all things singing, there is a balance to be struck.

So, there is singing dynamics and dynamic singing. The second includes the first, but the first does not include the second. Dynamic singing is about energy levels, volume levels, commitment to the spirit of the piece, and enhancement. And that takes singing to a different level altogether.

16

Pitch Perfect?

Let's talk tuning. Most people recognise without too much difficulty when someone (usually someone *else*) is singing out of tune. If they're not 'on the note', they are either flat or they're sharp. And singers will tie themselves in vocal and physical knots to 'sing in tune'. Often that means screwing their voices up (because the problem is usually flatness) in order to make a *sound* which is 'in tune', but which actually ends up being a noise which has ceased to be singing. Eyebrow-raising, cheek-lifting, mouth-pulling, buttock-clenching and lung-cramming are among the many contortions and excesses singers put themselves through. Sadly, none of these physical exertions lead to *singing* or to pitching a note accurately. The bottom line, indeed the only line, is that a singer will automatically sing in tune if their technique is secure. To underline the point and to avoid misunderstanding, out-of-tune singing is *bad* singing and, however great the voice or the singer, it is always *bad*. That is not to say that singers don't have off days, because contrary to some popular opinion, they really are human like the rest of us, but we are not talking here about the odd occasion or even the odd note, but about the general ability to sing in tune.

Singing out of tune is rarely a question of hearing. It is usually a matter of technique. If a singer is singing without energy, flabbily, then they are likely to be singing flat, like a string which is too slack for the pitch. If a singer is highly stressed or physically tense, the opposite is the case: they sing sharp, like an over-tightened string. We say that they are wound up like a clock spring. I have used the image of strings, but for strings, think vocal chords. If the chords are too slack for the pitch, the note will be flat; if they are too tight, the note will be sharp.

However, would that tuning were that simple! I remember that a survey was carried out into the pitch of instrumental and vocal soloists and the conclusion was that many soloists play or sing slightly sharp, consciously or unconsciously, in order to stand out against the accompaniment, whether orchestral or vocal. This slight sharpness is sometimes called brightness, and usually indicates a voice in which the higher, brighter resonances are dominant. Is that singing in tune? It does beg the question.

Recourse is often made to the piano to indicate whether a singer is singing flat or sharp. For much of the time the piano is a reasonable guide, but don't forget that it is well tempered. A keyboard player can't vary the pitch of his or her instrument in the same way as a wind or string player can. Piano pitch is a mean or average, one pitch fits all. Take the note E, for example (though it could be any note). The E which is at the bottom of an E major chord (at the root) is not the same E which is the major third in a C major chord. The major third is fractionally higher. The singer can (and should) make that adjustment, though in a singer with a musical ear it will just happen. If it doesn't, the chord sounds dull.

In a choir there is the additional headache of communal pitch. What can you do to rescue sagging pitch? Absolutely nothing, and certainly not by deliberately singing sharp, because *you* will be the one who sounds out of tune and looks silly. This is the bugbear of those with absolute (perfect) pitch.

So what is perfect pitch? In its most basic form, it is the ability to recognise or sing a note at the correct pitch without reference to a known tone. In other words, if a violin plays an Ab, the person with perfect pitch will be able to name it without being given another named note to compare it with. Or if a singer with perfect pitch is asked to sing an Eb, they can do so without the help of an instrument or tuning fork. Perfect pitch may be something people are born with or it may be a heightened aspect of memory, usually formed by early exposure to music and the names of notes. Most singers with perfect pitch I have known regard it as a disadvantage and try to switch it off or unlearn it. Relative pitch, on the other hand, is definitely worth having. This is an acquired skill, the result of high exposure to music, both heard and written, such that certain pitches become more or less perfectly memorised. Singers (as opposed to other musicians) often have relative pitch to a lesser or greater degree, because they rely on recognising the sensations of notes as part of their technique (see the chapter on Sensational Singing). A singer with relative pitch may say that a note sounds or feels like a C. Relative pitch may not work all the time as absolute pitch does, but in practical terms it is much more useful, as it has most of the advantages of perfect pitch but none of the disadvantages.

Singers with absolute pitch encounter difficulties with tuning deviations when singing with other people, when singing music which is transposed and when singing at period pitch (see below). Singers with relative pitch have a developed idea of pitch, but do not suffer from the cognitive dissonance experienced by singers with absolute pitch when tuning deviates from the norm (i.e. the expected). Singers with perfect pitch will be disturbed by the fact that they perceive music at baroque pitch as being played or sung 'in the wrong key', while singers with relative pitch will be aware that it feels different, but will grow accustomed to the change in sensations very quickly. The unease experienced by perfect-pitchers over baroque pitch suggests that cultural environment plays a large part in the development of perfect pitch, as presumably an 18th-century singer would have perfect pitch attuned to A=415, not A=440 as in contemporary pitch. There's a PhD there!

We also need to think of pitch in a global context

to stop us getting too precious about it. In the Western world, we think of a semitone as the smallest division of pitch, but in Eastern countries there are many more divisions. What may sound out of tune to Western ears may be perfectly acceptable to Eastern ears. In the Middle Eastern Hejaz scale, for instance, there are intervals of three semitones (does it make sense to have three halves in a whole?). Indian ragas often use intervals smaller than a semitone, and Arab *maqamat* music may use quarter-tone intervals. In both ragas and *maqamat*, the distance between a note and an inflection of that same note may be less than a semitone. There is even the term 'microtonal', and I don't need to tell you what means!

Then there is the wider question of pitch and its role in performance history. Without going into the academic niceties of whether there is such a phenomenon as 'authentic' pitch, whether it can be reliably defined in any one period and whether we should adopt it under any circumstances, current performance practice may require a singer to sing baroque music at A=415 rather than A=440; in other words, a semitone below contemporary pitch. For the singer with absolute pitch, seeing one written pitch and singing at another may require tiring mental gymnastics. And even for the singer without perfect pitch, the disjunction between sight and sound can be unsettling and affect technique. The problems are exacerbated if 'classical' pitch is used, because A=430 (a quarter-tone below modern pitch) falls fairly and squarely in the gaps, and singers with solid techniques will become disorientated and feel that they are singing flat. On the plus side, it may feel slightly easier. There has even been a campaign to sing Verdi at lower pitch, a fad adopted by the composer himself for a short time. It certainly does make life easier for many singers, but would cause practical mayhem if generally adopted.

It is also worth remembering that standardisation of pitch is relatively recent. As we have seen, pitch has tended to get higher with time, causing problems for singers. In 1859 France passed a law establishing the *diapason normal* (A=435). This was the first attempt at standardising pitch. In England we had the old philharmonic pitch at A=452, and then the new philharmonic pitch at A=439. It was up to each conductor and orchestra to decide which to use, which was an impossible situation for singers, who would sing the same work at one pitch here and another pitch there, often in consecutive performances. The picture was further clouded by English organs, which tended to be tuned high. If used in conjunction with an orchestra, the orchestra had to tune up. Finally in 1939 an international conference voted on A=440, which became known as concert pitch. Notwithstanding, minor pitch variations still exist across the world.

Different countries and different traditions have different tolerance levels when it comes to pitch. Here are some caricatures as examples. Listen to a Russian Orthodox choir. The church-music purist may hear nothing but a tendency towards descending pitch, and be deaf to the depth of sound and blind to the profound spirituality of the music-making. The same may be said of gospel choirs or Corsican new music, or any other folk music.

So, although singers must sing in tune, let's put tuning in context and not be too hasty to judge others, as though we never have off (key) days ourselves.

17

Sight-Singing

First of all, let me dispel some myths. Singers, and British singers in particular, get very hung up and precious about 'sight-reading'. Strictly speaking, you can only sight-read a piece once – the first time you see it. Thereafter, what counts is accurate reading coupled with hard work and repetition to learn a piece to performance standard. So, there is a difference between being a good sight-reader and being a good reader. There is also a difference (and a significant one) between being able to read the dots in rehearsals and being able to sing them accurately on the night. Ask yourself which singer better serves the composer. There is a further difference between the singer who sings accurately but mechanically, and the singer who sings the right notes from the heart. And yet another between the singer who has their head in the copy and the singer who has the copy in their head.

Sight-reading can become an obsession, and one

which is totally unrelated to the performance of the music. Those who are slower readers are often regarded as second-class singers (or, worse, second-class citizens), which is grossly unfair. If you are a quick reader and are frustrated by the slower pace of others, join another choir. Better still, examine where your priorities are and what music-making is really all about!

Then there is the whole question of singing from memory. To my mind that is a far more useful skill than sight-reading, but one which most amateur singers find extremely challenging, if not totally impossible. I suspect this is because they are rarely called upon to do it. There is a persuasive argument that you don't really know a piece unless you can sing it from memory. You only have to think of the impact of a gospel choir or a Welsh male voice choir or an opera chorus in full swing to hear and feel the extra dimension that singing from memory brings. Music cannot come off the page if your eyes are glued to it. Sadly, tragically, the musical life of the UK has been severely impoverished in recent years by an education system which has been forced to cut back on music provision in an utterly draconian and barbaric way. Such financial short-termism has appalling long-term consequences. The lack of classroom singing in many schools from primary level upward has had a knock-on effect on our ability to hear and memorise a tune without seeing the music. I know many adults who really struggle with singing from memory or picking up a tune without the music in front of them, the majority in fact, and it boils down to not having to do it. Cultures which pass on music orally have a great advantage over ours.

What we do have in this country is a great choral tradition, nourished and sustained by cathedral and college choirs, of which in many ways we can be rightly proud. However, this tradition's excellence comes at a cost, and the cost is vocal. Young and immature voices having to get their chords round a new anthem, *Mag* and *Nunc*,[8] psalms and responses each day run huge risks, both vocally and musically, as they distort their technique to get the right note out. The same can be true of mature voices in cathedral choirs unless their techniques are rock solid. It is significant that young singers from collegiate choirs who go on to music colleges have great difficulty in coming to terms with the demands of the training they receive and they have to spend a long time unlearning the bad habits they have acquired in the choir stalls, because the approach to singing is so different. Many singers never manage to shrug off completely the bad habits formed in their early years.

Therefore, good sight-reading does not necessarily mean good singing and, worse, often results in bad singing.

Singers often ask me to teach them to sight-read. Nine times out of ten the problem is not *primarily* that they can't read the dots (though that may also be true), but that they actually can't sing certain dots with technical confidence. If you're a soprano and you can't sing top F properly, then you're not going to able to read

8 Trade abbreviations for the *Magnificat* and *Nunc Dimittis*.

pieces with top Fs in them, because your technique is not up to it. You wouldn't expect a Grade 5 pianist to be able to sight-read a complex Chopin sonata, because they wouldn't have the technical skill to get their hands round the keyboard and their fingers on the right notes. Yet singers expect (and are expected) to be able to sight-read Bach when they struggle to sing a hymn or a folk tune with technical assurance. The expectation is unrealistic. You cannot expect to read confidently unless your technique allows you to sing the notes you see in front of you. This accounts for the note-blindness that occurs for many singers when a passage goes out of their technical comfort zone – most fall apart and grind to a halt. They may be confident in reading in the lower part of their voice, say, but unable to cope with notes in the upper part. So, being able to sight-read and being able to sing properly are two sides of the same coin. What tends to happen is that singers will force their voices in order to be able to 'sing' certain notes which they have not sorted out technically. But it's not really singing, and the more they do it, the more difficult it is to undo the 'knots' into which they tie their vocal chords.

To sum up, sight-reading is a useful skill, but it comes a long way down the list when it comes to making music; and to expect to sight-read before you can sing properly is (yet again) putting the cart before the horse.

18

Seeing is Reading

I discussed at some length in the last chapter the question of sight-reading. I am now going to look into the much more useful matter of reading music, whether for the first time or subsequently.

When singers ask me to help them with (what they refer to as) sight-reading, what they really mean is that they want to read music more efficiently, and that is a thoroughly good goal to work towards. However, I find my response to their request really difficult to formulate. To start with, singers often imagine exercises and 'methods' designed to improve reading. My reaction has always been that working through that sort of designated material is monumentally boring and that my time can be better spent on helping singers with other aspects of singing. I know that sounds arrogant and dismissive, so let me explain.

Reading music as an instrumentalist and reading

music as a singer are two very different processes, although there is a good deal of common ground as well. I touched earlier on the question of reading being limited by a singer's technical ability. If a singer can't sing a certain note and the music includes it, they are not going to be able to sing it at all and therefore they won't be able to read it, because if they are worrying about how to sing the note the worry will cloud their ability to read. The mental process may well be more complex than that, but that is the gist of it.

When you think about it, for singers the whole process of reading music is extreme multitasking! You have to read notes, words, signs and symbols, look at the conductor, hold the copy and engage technique to produce sound, all in one and the same split second. Not only that, but you have to look ahead to see what's coming and keep going if you make a slip. That involves several parts of the brain working together at the same time, and some people simply can't do that. It's like rubbing your stomach with one hand and patting your head with the other. It's jolly difficult, and being able to do it has absolutely nothing to do with intelligence. You might compare it to driving. When you start to learn to drive, there seem to be more things required of you than your brain can cope with: depress the clutch, engage the gear, look in the mirror, signal, steer, look at the road signs, the other road users, watch out for the unexpected, look ahead. You can see the parallels. But for most people the component parts of driving gradually become second nature and happen automatically. It takes practice and it takes lessons, but people do get there in the end. Singing is very much like that.

Therefore, however hard singing in a choir is, most people *can* improve. One way is to discipline yourself to keep going after making a mistake. This always reminds me of *Mastermind*. The best contestants are the ones who, if they get an answer wrong or can't answer, immediately put it out of their minds and carry on with the next question. The flip side is that you see others who have not acquired that knack still thinking about Question 1 when they're supposed to be thinking about Question 2 or 3. All singers make mistakes. Don't let a mistake hold you back, and I mean that musically as well as metaphorically.

Singers need to 'live in the moment', that is, not dwell on what is past and only look far enough ahead to prepare for the next note or phrase. Just as you can see some *Mastermind* contestants still thinking, several questions on, about the answer they didn't know, so you can see singers, certainly professionals, thinking about that difficult note or passage, often pages in advance. If you know what to listen for, you can hear the singer start to lose confidence bars ahead, because they are worrying about the big moment yet to come. Fatal. That's where living in the moment is such an important discipline. Humour helps, too. Making a mistake should not be the cause of guilt and shame. Learning by making mistakes or by trying things out is what rehearsals are for. And if you make a mistake in a performance, ask yourself which is better: the singer who stops and crumples into a heap or the one who mentally shrugs it off and keeps going?

I want to offer my personal experience as an encouragement to those who want to improve their reading, although they should not necessarily take mine as an example to emulate! I had very little formal musical training at school. I had a year of piano lessons with the old lady across the road and hated them. I learnt the cello up to Grade 3 at school and then stopped to concentrate on public exams (and lugging the cello around on the bus was a pain). I didn't do O Level (GCSE) music. I did play the recorder (I think the whole class was taught at primary school), and I did teach myself to play guitar chords from the Bert Weedon guitar book. Later I transferred the guitar chords to the piano and put the melody on top. I did sing in the school choir, but remember being totally at sea when I took part in large choral events outside the school and I often ended up pages out. So, how did it happen that I went on to sing in cathedral choirs for nine years and was an ad hoc (an occasional singer) for the BBC Singers? It was a question of rolling up my sleeves, so to speak, and getting down to hard graft – without the aid of a book. I bashed out the tune on the piano and worked at singing the notes correctly. And the process was long and often painful.

I know other singers who have been through music college and who didn't really knuckle down to acquiring good reading skills until they had to. If you can get away with it, you will! That's human nature. One of my professional students did sit down eventually with a book, but worked at it on her own, because she knew her income depended on it.

One of the problems I used to find very hard to understand in singers, particularly choir singers, was a lack of sense of rhythm, until one of my pupils had an epiphany in the middle of the night (so he told me). Choir singers rely on the conductor so much for leads and difficult rhythms that they find it very difficult to cope when singing on their own with no-one waving their arms in front of them. Take the stick away and they fall down. Now, one can argue until the cows come home that this should not be so, but we have to accept that it is reality for many singers. Orchestral musicians seem far better at it, probably because their control of their instruments is more direct.

So how can singers be helped to stand on their own two feet rhythmically? A basic knowledge of note values and time signatures is essential and that is a matter of hard graft, but even when singers know those things in their heads it doesn't mean that they won't fall into the same traps every time they sing a particular passage of music.

In my experience, in order to improve rhythm to the point of self-reliance, the first thing to do is to get into the discipline of marking the copy clearly and efficiently. I used not to look at my pupils' copies, but, when eventually I did, I was astonished by the way they had marked them. When I suggested some clearer ways, many of their rhythmic difficulties disappeared immediately. It is a question of annotating the copy in a way which helps you see the wood for the trees.

Unless you have been taught how to mark up copies, either formally or by sitting next to someone in the know and who is willing to help, how could you possibly know?

Another major help is being able to beat, tap or click in time to the music. That sounds easy, but many singers find it incredibly difficult and their embarrassment at not being very good at it makes them reluctant to keep making the effort. Choose a straightforward piece of music which you know well – a hymn, for instance (plenty on YouTube) – have the music in front of you and click your fingers, tap or clap your way through it. Be aware of the places where you get left behind or where you get in front, and keep trying until you get it right, always bearing in mind that music, even in repetitive hymns, needs a certain amount of flexibility in the performance. For this reason, a metronome can be very useful for instilling the basic rhythm of a piece, but it won't be quite the same in performance, where one hopes that the music will breathe a bit. There are many free metronome apps available for mobile phones, so there is no excuse these days.

The tapping/clicking is one step towards internalising the rhythm, to feeling in your bones the march of time. With disciplined practice this should become instinctive, so that you will need to click only in particularly difficult rhythmic passages. A good sense of rhythm is especially useful when notes are tied across a bar line or a phrase starts on an offbeat or there is a hemiola (where you get a feeling of two in a three time-frame). You need to be able to feel a clear rhythmic pulse in order to go across it or feel the beat after it. I remember (as many singers will) that the great choral conductor, the late Sir David Willcocks, used to stamp his foot hard on the main beat of a bar in order to get singers to come in promptly the beat after. Never to be forgotten.

I have recently come across an American publication[9] which contains over four hundred pages of musical examples designed to guide singers through the process of reading. I would say that there are five exercises on average per page, which gives about two thousand examples in total! It is an invaluable resource, the best I've seen, but it doesn't come cheap, though you may be lucky enough (as I was) to pick up a reasonably priced second-hand copy. The first stage is rhythm only; only beats are indicated, no key signatures. The best approach seems to be to *say* the notes to 'lah' (or whatever), holding them for the right length, then to graduate to singing the rhythm on a single vowel and on a single note. And I suggest doing it to a metronome beat. The best advice is to keep going, even if you go wrong.

It is perfectly logical to establish a strong sense of rhythm before going on to the challenge of pitching intervals. At the very least it cuts down the number

9 *Music for Sight Singing* by Robert W. Ottman and Nancy Rogers, published Pearson Prentice Hall.

of problems facing a singer who cannot cope with the multitasking involved in reading music.

So here are some practical ways of going about it and getting down to it:

1. You do need to learn some basics: time signatures, key signatures, note values, intervals and musical instructions (usually in Italian).

2. Basic keyboard skills make the whole process much easier. Bashing out your line on the piano with one finger is absolutely fine.

3. One very important part of the process is feeling the pulse of the music, the onward march of the beat, the march of time, marking time. That expression is a reminder that soldiers marched to the beat of a drum; they moved forward in step to the beat, and that is what we are doing as singers: singing along to the beat in a body as one. In practice you need to be able to feel the beat through your body and particularly in your hands, so that, when you need to, you can tap or clap or click your fingers to reinforce the beat. Many singers find this really difficult, but it is fundamental and it will come with practice. Clicking or tapping during rehearsals is likely to infuriate your neighbours, but you can finger-tap silently and unobtrusively against the copy or against your body.

4. Or try singing something simple against a metronome, tapping at the same time. You will probably find that you get out of sync with the metronome, because music is rarely absolutely rigid, but it is a good discipline to be able to sing and tap to an inflexible beat.

5. If you can bash out the tune on a piano, all well and good, but then test yourself by singing unaccompanied and checking against the piano from time to time. You don't really know a piece unless you can sing it unaided.

6. Practise reading short, simple tunes you don't know. A traditional hymn book is a good source of material or a book of traditional folk songs. Don't bother about the words at first. Just sing the tune to any vowel or vowel combination you like and take as long as you need to. Then when you can sing the tune at the right speed, try adding the words.

7. Something which seems to trip up a lot of singers is when a single vowel or syllable is sung over two or more notes, which is a very common occurrence in vocal music. An example might be the first line of *Rule, Britannia!*: *When Britain fir-ir-ir-ir-irst at Heaven's command*. This is known in music-speak as a melisma and is indicated by a slur above the notes on the page and dashes in the text. The difficulty singers have is, I suspect, again to do with technique,

because sustaining a single vowel across several notes takes courage as well as skill. I have no quick fix for this. It's a matter of seeing the slur and having the courage to observe it. But be aware that a slur can also be a phrase mark and does not necessarily signify a melisma.

8. Don't expect choir rehearsals alone to prepare you for the concert. You must work on the score yourself and prepare for each rehearsal by looking through those passages where you know you are having problems. Don't just sing through the easy bits; work at the hard ones!

9. If you have difficulty finding a note for a particular entry, look in the score to see if you can get that note from somewhere else: another vocal part or in the accompaniment. Then put a ring round that note and a ring round your entry with a line joining them. That will remind you of the thought process.

10. Singers often have difficulty keeping going from one musical system to another or from one page to another, because it involves looking at the music ahead or turning the page while singing the bar or the note before. And this problem occurs not just on the first reading, but on many subsequent ones. Get into the habit of memorising the bar before the change of system or the turnover. Over time that thought process will become second nature. Draw a

pair of glasses in the score at the end of a system or the end of a page to remind you to look ahead. Or write in at the end of one page the next notes and words on the following page to give yourself time to turn over. Or just write *TURN* or *OVER* or *VS* (from the Italian *volti subito* – turn quickly).

11. If you are having trouble with a particular passage, try learning it off by heart, as the notes on the page can often (paradoxically) get in the way.

12. Arrows (vertical in either direction) are useful reminders for places where you are in the habit of not going high or low enough. They can also be used to indicate pitch, although, as I have said earlier, singing in tune is not a matter of correct hearing, but of correct technique. If the technique is right, the tuning will be right.

13. Arrows (horizontal, pointing to the right in the direction of the music) are used to remind the singer to carry on through the phrase or perhaps not to breathe in an obvious place.

14. Circle or underline notes, words or instructions you trip over or ignore more than twice. Or mark in felt tip (only if the score belongs to you).

15. A tick is usually a breath mark: breathe here.

16. If you want to mark in beats of the bar, write them clearly in numerals above your part over the main beats of the bar. You can also put in vertical lines if the rhythm is complicated to show you where the main beats are in comparison with the offbeat notes you have to sing.

17. Use sharp, flat and natural signs if you have difficulty pitching/finding the note.

18. It is sometimes helpful to think of an awkward or confusing interval in a different way from the way in which the composer has written it. If you are singing a piece in D major and there is a jump from F# to Bb, it may help you to think of the Bb as an A#. This does involve mental gymnastics, but it can help you see the wood for the trees.

19. If you have a long gap before your next entry, write in the page number where you next sing and turn to it in advance.

20. Marking the score is absolutely crucial to getting the music right. Singers' scores are (and should be) littered with markings. If yours aren't, it's high time they were!

21. As a result of the amazing technology that is now readily available and within most people's budgets, many choirs produce sound material to help their

members learn the dots. Typically, this might be a recording of a particular vocal line played on the piano. For those without keyboard skills or access to a keyboard, this is invaluable for private practice and with earphones you can take the recording anywhere. Whenever possible, I would recommend looking at the score at the same time as listening to the sound file in order to reinforce the link between the aural and the visual. I would also encourage singers to use the sound file to learn their own line and then to sing it against the other parts, perhaps using a commercial recording. Just listening, though, is not enough. It has to be active listening. You won't learn just by absorption; you have to try to be one step ahead of the recording and be able to sing the notes on the page in your head (i.e. without making sound).

22. Conductors can also increase the confidence of their choir members by mixing up voice parts in rehearsals or by having singers walk randomly around the room while singing. This will be very scary at first for some, but it is worth going through the pain barrier. Obviously it is designed to reduce a singer's reliance on their neighbour and increase their self-confidence.

23. You can't look too much or too often at the score (in advance of the performance). Maria Callas cited as an example the man who had helped her so much,

the great conductor Tullio Serafin, who would spend the night before a performance poring over scores he had conducted many times before, because he would always see something he had missed or undervalued or overemphasized in the past. Toscanini did the same. The learning process never stops. And, if a work of art, great or small, visual or aural, really is great, then we should be able to return to it time and again and find new inspiration, and all the more so with the advance of age. What we saw as being of unequivocal importance in our twenties may seem of little or only secondary interest in our sixties.

19

Interpretation: Joining Up the Dots

Singing should be fun, but that does not mean that it is frivolous. Singers have a responsibility to respect the composer's work and perform it as faithfully and as sensitively as they can.

In order to understand what you see on the page, to convey it in and through your voice and to communicate it to an audience, a singer needs to be aware of the way a composer composes. Composers of vocal music *usually* start with a text – one they have commissioned, one they have chosen because it appeals to them, one that has been stipulated by a promoter or sponsor or one they have made up themselves. Therefore, it follows that the music they write is an expression of what they feel about the words, how they respond to the text.

A composer first hears the music in his head and/or

has it at his fingertips, and then transfers what he hears onto paper. Then the composer has to try to make clear to the performer (who has not had the music in his head) how the music is to be played and sung in the way the composer conceived it. This is an area of potential confusion and misunderstanding. Communication between people in everyday speech is tricky enough, but the language of music is an artificial construct and something which has to be learnt. What's more, printed music using traditional notation is a semi-permanent, visual representation of something intangible, invisible and fleeting. Take the example of the folk songs collected by Vaughan Williams, Cecil Sharp and others at the turn of the 20th century. They went into town and country, prospecting for local tunes. When they came across a folk song which they considered worthy of being preserved, in the absence of portable sound-recording equipment, they wrote it down on paper using traditional notation, trying to capture what they heard as best as their ears and the musical form would allow. The formal division of music into bars with regular time signatures is at odds with music learnt and transmitted orally and then performed as occasion demands or as whim leads. Speeds had to be indicated by formal metronome marks. Guidance about expression had to be given in words, most likely Italian ones (another barrier to comprehension). Already the number of symbols and instructions has multiplied between hearing the music in the field and noting it down in the study. What started out as live music in a state of perpetual re-creation ends up frozen on the page. It is the singer's job to thaw it, to work out what the composer originally heard in his head and tried to convey on paper, to fill in any gaps by using their own imagination and to bring the music to life again in performance. If it weren't for performers, music would not get off the page: it would remain silent and, to all intents and purposes, would be dead.

The process of understanding music of all genres and periods for performance purposes works fundamentally in the same way. We have to learn to read the signposts the composer gives us on the page, know something of the musical tradition he is/was working in, and build that knowledge into the limitations of our own performing ability, filtered through our own artistic personality. Great artists respect the composer and the composition, while bringing something special of their own to the performance, a je ne sais quoi. That is how music lives. Performance cannot be set in stone (or on CD). There is no such thing as a definitive performance, because we know that successive generations of musicians will produce the next definitive performance! The singer has to re-create the composer's intentions (in so far as it is possible to identify them) every time he performs.

Music only exists (that is, it is only accessible to most people) through the medium of performance; the score reaches the audience by coming off the page via the performer. This necessarily involves compromise. For instance, a singer with a big voice may have to sing a piece more slowly than a singer with a lighter voice. A singer with a fertile artistic imagination may be able to bring a piece to life in a more interesting way than a singer who approaches the piece more literally. That is the glory and also the grief of being an artistic medium: bringing music back from the dead does not come without risk.

Only a solo unaccompanied singer has complete freedom of interpretation and total licence of expression. As soon as a singer is joined by other singers or musicians, interpretation becomes collaboration. Think of a singer and an accompanist. They have to work on a piece and agree how to perform it together. That doesn't mean that something new and unrehearsed won't emerge during performance, but it should be within the framework the two artists have established beforehand; they should be so sensitive to each other's artistry that, mysteriously and wonderfully, they move and feel as one. Now scale up that situation to a conductor, a choir, an orchestra and soloists. What a pulling in opposite directions that can be! Of course, it is the conductor's job to bring all forces into line, so that they move together in the same direction. Individuality has to be tempered for the common good. That is a danger point for singers. How much can you subsume your uniqueness without losing your vocal integrity?

So, how should a singer approach a score? Most singers will rush straight to the music, because that is what drives them. But the singer's first duty is surely to read and understand the text, work out what it means to them personally in order to better understand what the composer thinks about it and why he has set it in the way he has. Understanding the text and being thoroughly familiar with it, even if it doesn't come first in the discovery process, is essential. That process is easier if the text is in the singer's native tongue. If not, the work involved is much greater and more painstaking, but nonetheless essential.

So, read through the text, read it out loud, experiment with ways of expressing it – without uttering a note. Sometimes, the piece may be inspired by a landscape or a painting or a love affair or an event. Find out about them – the knowledge will enhance your understanding and enrich your performance.

Then look at the score. Does the way the composer has set the text surprise you in any way? It may contradict your own view of the text or extend it or deepen it. Or is it as you might have expected? Pay close attention to the composer's markings to see what he is telling you about his interpretation.

Singers tend to concentrate naturally on their own vocal line. But it is also important for the singer to know how he fits into the piece as a whole, and to listen to the accompaniment underneath the vocal line.

Try comparing different composers' settings of the same text. Housman poems were set by Butterworth, Vaughan Williams and Somervell, all within ten years of each other, and each composer took a very different approach. Both Puccini and Leoncavallo wrote operas based on Murger's *Scènes de la vie de bohème*. Puccini's *La Bohème* is now firmly part of the opera repertoire, whereas Leoncavallo's is only occasionally wheeled out as a curiosity. They are very different treatments. Schubert, Schumann and Wolf all set Goethe's *Wer sich der Einsamkeit ergibt*, admittedly across a period of some seventy years. Compare Haydn's own settings of the Mass (each very different), or Bach's own settings of the Passion; compare them with Masses and Passions by other composers. A singer, whether soloist or choir member, needs to have some understanding of why the work was written and what their role is within it.

Are composers' markings sacred? While we must treat the composer's intentions with the greatest respect, markings cannot always be set in stone if music is to live. A work may have been composed for a specific venue or with particular performers in mind. If you perform the same work in a larger or smaller venue, different performance criteria might have to come into play. In a larger space, speeds may have to be modified to cope with a more generous acoustic and therefore metronome markings may have to be stretched. Some parts, vocal or orchestral, may need reinforcing, because otherwise they may be lost. Is it better to play Bach on modern instruments or not at all? Should you play Bach organ music using romantic stops which were unknown in Bach's day? I remember George Thalben-Ball, distinguished long-serving organist at the Temple Church in London, playing Bach on the organ in Salisbury Cathedral and breaking every period law in the book by choosing stops and registrations which post-dated Bach, but my goodness, he made the piece, the organ and the audience sit up! The revival of period instruments and 'authentic' performance has re-opened our ears to very different soundscapes. This has been a wonderfully refreshing experience, to the extent that some people can no longer bear to listen to older music played on modern instruments. But that does not make it wrong to use modern instruments, especially if the alternative is silence.

And what about pitch? Baroque pitch is half a tone lower than modern pitch (A=415, not 440). How does that affect modern voices? See Chapter 16: Pitch Perfect? for a deeper discussion.

On rare occasions it is hard to escape the conclusion that a composer has made an error of judgement. It happens less now that compositions can be workshopped before being premiered or published. But what about the metronome marking which is so fast as to make the piece unplayable or unsingable at the printed speed? Or the underlay (the way notes are allocated to syllables) which simply doesn't work for the singer? There are examples in Handel's *Messiah*! Or the translation which doesn't make sense (Haydn's *Creation*)? Composers don't always know best.

And a lot of printed music contains errors or markings which don't stack up: the change in speed which was clearly intended to last a few bars only, but which the composer has not countermanded in the score with an a tempo; the hairpin which has no counterpart.

Each composer tries to exert lesser or greater control over the performer through the score. Puccini and Elgar knew exactly what they wanted and often wrote several markings over every bar. Verdi knew that singers have a tendency to sing too loudly and wrote *pppp*, not as a literal volume level, but as a restraint! Others are content to let the performer have their head. Yet others give phrase markings which are obvious to most performers and don't really need to be there. Some expect performers to take the lead and weave their own magic around the notes. In earlier music there may be no signposts at all or very few. Or there may be markings which are editorial and therefore totally subjective. These need to be approached with caution and can be legitimately ignored if a performer feels strongly that they run counter to their own interpretation.

All of which points to the conclusion that performance should be an intelligent and sensitive collaboration between composer and performer(s), taking into account space, time and circumstance, arguably in that order. Performance is severely impoverished if it does not go beyond a slavish and thoughtless observation of the markings on the page.

20

Warming Up or Cooling Down?

'Warming up' is a familiar term which is used in a number of languages (French, Italian and German, among many others). It is sometimes also referred to as vocalisation. But what does it mean?

Athletes warm up, too, and for the same reason as singers: to tone up their muscles, gradually and systematically, through exercise. You wouldn't get out of bed and run a marathon without any previous training, preparation or limbering up, so why sing without training or warming up?

Singers do vocal exercises for two reasons:

1. To warm their voices up.

2. To develop their technique.

I have to declare straight away that I am sceptical about

the *vocal* value of choir warm-ups. Exercising without really understanding what the exercise is aimed at and, more importantly, how to achieve it, can do more harm than good. Choir warm-ups may be good for team-building and developing a communal sense of purpose, and they may be good fun (nothing wrong with that), but in purely vocal terms they are very limited, precisely because they are undertaken by so many individuals at one time. And, sadly, they have become a tick-box activity for choirs, led in some cases by those who have enthusiasm in spades (which is important), but little understanding.

Choir warm-ups often include non-vocal exercises. These typically include breathing, physical movement and general loosening up. The caveats of the previous paragraph apply, and Chapter 2 on breathing will shed useful light here. What really counts is physical and mental alertness, the energy you need to sing. With practice it is possible to induce a state of alertness, even if you are feeling totally exhausted after the exertions of the day, but I am doubtful about the effectiveness of trying to recreate that state en masse. For introverts it may have the opposite effect: communal switching-on may become an individual turn-off.

As far as technical development is concerned, the best exercises are those which encourage the singer to develop the principles of technique without always singing the same tune(s). It is very tempting for singers to master a particular exercise only to find that they get stuck in the rut of doing the exercise in the same way.

The ultimate aims of singing technique are the freedom and flexibility to be able to interpret as the music dictates and as the singer wishes. Good vocal habits are cultivated by applying the same principles to different tunes and melodies. So, don't fall into the trap of believing that one set of exercises holds the key to a perfect technique. It can't and won't.

Exercises for vocal development are usually designed to concentrate on one or two aspects of singing at a time, say, one vowel or sequence of vowels or a vowel plus a consonant or one musical figure or an interval. In other words, the variables are reduced in comparison with singing a piece which has a whole range of words and notes. Exercises may consist of legato, staccato, vowels, consonants or actual words in any language. Regardless of the nature of the exercise, it is important to exercise a little and then rest, exercise a little and then rest. The gaps between exercises are as important as the exercises themselves, as they allow the muscles to relax. The bull-in-the-china-shop approach to warming up often results in hoarseness and strain.

But, as with all aspects of singing, there are dangers.

It is often said that humming is a useful warm-up activity and, although I don't use it regularly myself, there may be some gain in it. However, it is not that simple. For a start, there are two separate consonants which can be used for humming and one combination: M, N and NG, each producing different resonances in different areas. I strongly advise steering clear of N and NG until your technique is relatively secure. These are both nasal sounds and can easily drag the sound column off course into the nose, destroying the beauty of tone through excessive nasality. An M hum is perhaps more useful, but bear in mind that consonants (including M) travel with the sound column. If you are encouraged to hum with your mouth tightly closed and then open onto a vowel, the beam will again be knocked off course. In fact, if there is any facial tightness involved in producing the hum, it does more harm than good. What you might call a 'loose hum', which is really more vibrational than anything else, can be used to good effect, but it needs careful guidance (on column principles) and I would be very wary about doing it in a choir warm-up. It can be useful to sing an M consonant with a vowel (M-AH, M-EE, etc.), but the guiding image must be of the consonant on top of the sound column rising with the vowel into the head (where it is a long way away from the lips and the front of the face where a hum naturally occurs). There has to be a reason why singers singing the *Humming Chorus* in *Madama Butterfly* often open the hum discreetly into a vowel as the music rises!

Another potential disadvantage is that exercises per se have no emotional content and, as the voice thrives on emotion, there is the danger that an important dimension of the voice will be missing. The answer is to create one. Each tune has its own mood – happy or sad, for instance – and what may seem a small emotional input is enough. Or try singing an exercise in different moods. Aggression and/or anger are often useful emotions to harness, even if you are not an aggressive or angry person. The energy behind the emotion will bring that extra something to the sound which no amount of pure technique will. Aggression can also be harnessed to help singers find the right energy level needed for singing. If I ask a singer to sing a lyrical piece aggressively, their voice comes alive. The art lies in singing lyrical or quiet passages with the same underlying aggressive energy, but deploying it in a way which suits the music.

If I ask a singer to imagine a situation or an emotion during an exercise, the singing takes on an extra dimension which would be impossible to create by technique alone. Think of technique as the plastic housing around an electricity cable. It guides the electricity and connects source to target, but, unless there is a current running through it, the bulb at the end doesn't light up. If there is no emotion going through the technique, there is no illumination of the piece and neither the performer nor the audience is lit up.

In spite of what I have said about variety, it is also true that singers do have their favourite exercises which get their voices on track, even when (or perhaps especially when) they are suffering from a cold or exhaustion or something else which affects performance. Singers may also use phrases from operas, songs or oratorios for similar reasons. It is often the sequence of vowels which is beneficial; some phrases almost sing themselves, while others, where the vowel sequence is less vocal, are hard work. If you listen to singers vocalising backstage before a performance, you will hear a bewildering variety of warm-up techniques. Ultimately what matters is what makes *your* voice work (which is another of my reservations about choir warm-up sessions).

The ideal, of course, is that singers should warm up on their own before arriving at the rehearsal in advance of a choir warm-up. Even five minutes in the car (preferably stationary) is better than nothing. But as important is to get used to the idea that singing requires energy and that you need to acquire the knack of 'switching on' every time you sing. Switch on the ignition and allow the engine time to warm up. The aim is to be physically relaxed (not limp!), mentally alert and energy-charged.

21

Vocal Health

In this chapter I am going to leave aside technique and explore other factors which may affect your voice. Please note that I am not a doctor and that I am giving a layman's overview of the subject. If you think you may have a problem, please see your doctor.

Your voice is part of you and it is affected by your moods and emotions, your general well-being, your hearing, what you eat and drink, whether you're tired, whether you smoke, and whether you have a cold.

If you get out of bed feeling sluggish, out of sorts, under par, and you have to sing, what can you do? Performers in all fields often have routines which they follow in an almost ritualistic way, believing that ritual observance will see them through. And they may be right. If that works for you and it's not too quirky and not injurious to health, then fine. Such rituals typically include eating certain foods (and not others), taking certain medications, reading certain books, putting on certain clothes or preparing for a performance in the same way each time. The familiarity of such routines probably helps to calm singers down and take their minds off the fact that they are not feeling a hundred per cent. Warm up, but warm up slowly, in short bursts, across a small range first, and don't expect too much of your voice or yourself. Don't warm up so much that you use up all your energy (and voice) before the performance. Pace yourself. If you have practised the mental switching-on as you take in the breath to sing, the adrenaline will probably carry you through the performance.

It is important to bear in mind that very few singers are 'on song', on tip-top form, every time they sing. In fact, the reverse is true: they rarely are, and that goes for professionals just as much as it does for amateurs.

What if you have a cold or sore throat? Some colds in the early stages can actually help the voice. Singers often sing very well the day before they go down with a cold. In fact, some regard it as axiomatic that, if they are singing well one day, they will get a cold the next. My guess is that the beginnings of a cold block some resonators and that the sound gets redirected to others which may not usually come into play. That may be a simplistic explanation unsupported by medical science, but, even so, some colds can certainly improve resonation. If the cold is a head cold, then steaming in the old-fashioned way – head under a towel over a bowl of hot water, perhaps with salt or friar's balsam or Olbas Oil – is a simple but effective method for alleviating the symptoms. Sore throats may be treated by gargling with warm salty water, but this is of limited benefit. Sucking sweets may also make you feel better without necessarily curing the cause. If the condition is so bad that you simply can't get a note out, then not singing (cancelling if it's a performance) is the only sensible option.

Steroids have become magic remedies for many singers. *If you have to go on, get your doctor to prescribe steroids*, runs the wisdom. But it is not wisdom; it is the opposite – extremely *un*wise. Steroids are at best an in extremis sticking-plaster solution, because they are used to reduce swelling in any part of the body, not specifically the vocal chords. Therefore, if steroids are used regularly (even if for non-vocal reasons), the singer runs the risk of side effects, notably the deepening or heightening of the vocal range. But, if a singer has to resort to steroids on a regular basis, there is likely to be something very wrong with their technique which causes the chords to swell. If that is not addressed, their singing life may be severely curtailed.

If you find that you are persistently hoarse after singing, you need to see a singing teacher *and* an ear, nose and throat (ENT) specialist immediately, as something must be wrong physically, probably caused by poor vocal technique. There are a number of possible explanations for this condition. It *may* be a hardness or growth on the edge of the vocal chords, caused by the chords coming together more violently than they normally should. This might be the result of vocal abuse (excessive shouting[10] or strained singing) or even persistent coughing. There are several forms of growth including nodules, polyps and cysts. None of these are cancerous. Treatment varies from complete vocal rest to voice therapy to surgery (most often, these days, by laser).

While it is true that hoarseness is one of the symptoms of cancer of the larynx, it can also be a result of acid reflux, where acid comes back up the windpipe onto the vocal chords, which then swell as a result of the irritation. A common description is that the acid reflux 'burns' the vocal chords (it can also cause heartburn). A variety of avoidance techniques can be used. By the by, isn't it bizarre that singing badly has become a socially acceptable norm in some situations? It is often more 'in' to sing yourself hoarse at a football match than to sing properly.

A less damaging condition, though still an intrusive one, is postnasal drip. This occurs when 'stuff' from your nose and sinuses drips into the back of your nose and then onto your vocal chords. Saline washes (gargling with salt) and antihistamine products are often prescribed. The condition may also be brought on by allergic reactions of all kinds, including against pollen.

Singers often say that certain foods, notably dairy products (e.g. milk, cheese and chocolate), 'clog' or 'fur' their throats. Medical opinion is divided on this issue, but, if that is what you think, then avoid those foods

10 I have known cases where uncontrolled shouting at football matches or in the classroom has seriously affected the vocal chords.

before singing. Eating a large meal before singing is also unwise, as it will make you feel weighed down at a time when you want to feel buoyant and energetic. It is important to drink enough liquid to keep the body, including the vocal chords, hydrated. Tea, coffee and Coke contain caffeine, which tends to dehydrate the body by increasing urine production. Water at room temperature is generally reckoned the best hydrator for singers. Care is needed to get the right balance between adequate hydration and getting 'caught short' on stage!

Incidentally, sometimes when singers have to cough, the tickle in the throat is not caused by dust or some other foreign body, but by the muscles in the larynx objecting when the vocal adjustment is not quite right. Singers often reach for the water bottle at this point, probably pointlessly. It is not unusual for singers to experience this sensation while their technique is developing, because they don't always get it right.

As for alcohol before or, worse, during singing, don't even think about it. Just as alcohol will affect any human activity in an abnormal way, so anything that affects your body unnaturally should be avoided while singing. And that includes drinking alcohol for 'Dutch courage'. You may think you're singing better after a drink, but you're probably not. It is more likely that *you* feel you're singing better, but no-one else hears it that way. And alcohol will dry out your system. If you suffer from nerves, then there are other ways of controlling them. I have known singers take beta blockers to get them through in times of stress, but these should be seen as a temporary solution only.

I have also known singers, some of them very good ones, who smoke. They may smoke to calm their nerves, but, as we all know, smoking is addictive and anything addictive or potentially addictive should be avoided. It is playing with fire, in this case literally. Just think of where the smoke goes: mouth, nose, throat, vocal chords, larynx, windpipe, lungs – in other words, it passes through all of the component parts of the voice. Inhalation of smoke from cigarettes, cigars and pipes, whether self-inflicted or second-hand, brings high risk of vocal damage and cancer. Irritation of the chords, excess mucus, damage to the lungs and throat cancer are all possible consequences. If you do smoke, please seek help to give it up. I have known singers of all ages whose voices are audibly affected by smoking. And it should go without saying that the same health warning applies to drug abuse.

Blocked sinuses may be a temporary or permanent condition, but one which can affect the voice significantly. In extreme cases, I have known singers have operations on their sinuses with amazingly beneficial results.

Singers are sensitive people, that is part of their artistic nature, and they are prone to psychosomatic illness. A psychosomatic disorder is the outward physical manifestation of emotional distress or inner trauma. The physical symptoms are very real, but often defy medical diagnosis. Singers, especially at the start of their careers, are known to fall sick before concerts or auditions. Anxiety about the event brings on a psychosomatic episode. This syndrome usually disappears with time and experience, but medical and/or psychological help may be necessary in some persistent cases.

You often hear people say that they are 'tone-deaf'. What they usually mean is that they are convinced that they can't hold a tune or sing in tune, although the term actually means the inability to distinguish between notes of different pitches; tone-deafness is the aural equivalent of colour blindness. However, most people who say they're tone-deaf are physically capable of singing in tune, but they lack the discipline, effort or training to do so. There may be many reasons for this, but the usual ones are that they are afraid of appearing silly when they sing (ironically when they sing properly!) and that they have no reason to address the matter. Listen to them speak. If you hear a variation in pitch and tone in their speaking voice, it is more than likely that they can sing. If they speak in an absolutely deadpan voice, with no variation in pitch at all, on a monotone, then possibly they are 'tone-deaf', i.e. their vocal organs are incapable of reproducing changes in pitch or are so atrophied through lack of use that a seismic shift is necessary.

I often come across singers with varying degrees of hearing loss. Many tend to direct the sound to where they can hear it better… or where they *think* they can hear it better. If one ear is worse than the other, they will tend to aim the sound towards the good ear. You may be able to see this in a singer's face: a tendency to screw up the face or skew the mouth in order to direct the sound towards the better ear. This often means compromised resonance and falsification of sound. Depending on the nature of the deafness, a singer may subconsciously increase the higher frequencies of their voice so that it is easier for *them* to hear, resulting in an over-bright voice with excessive cut or blade, lacking in natural depth, warmth and beauty. These telltale physical signs may indicate to the teacher that there is a hearing problem which the singer may not even be aware of. Hearing aids, however sophisticated, may make it hard for a singer to hear what their voice is doing, both internally and externally. Care and patience are needed to re-educate such singers about what sounds right and what to listen for.

In cases of severe deafness, tuning may be affected. If a singer has a solid technique and is used to relying on sensation rather than sound, it is possible to overcome or compensate for hearing loss and there are examples of professional singers whose careers have continued in spite of disability. I think particularly of the hugely inspiring mezzo Janine Roebuck. Sadly, there are examples of others who, in spite of being first-rank singers, have not been able to carry on. The wonderful Cornish baritone Benjamin Luxon is one of the best-known examples.

The condition known as tinnitus, where the sufferer hears a permanent ringing sound or an intermittent noise over which they have no control, may not be a problem in mild cases because you can train the brain to filter the noise out, but in extreme cases the interference may be impossible to ignore. What's more, it may distort or destroy the singer's perception of pitch.

Just as menstruation, pregnancy and the menopause affect different women in different ways generally, so these hormonal changes affect singing in different ways too. Some singers starting or going through their monthly cycle will exhibit less ease at the top of the voice and may possibly experience a reduction in range (by a note or two), less flexibility, hoarseness and less stamina. Others show some or none of these. I understand that this is connected with fluid retention in the vocal chords and there is nothing you can do to reduce this. What you can do is box clever. Take on board what your typical symptoms are and get round them by adapting the way you use your voice (if in rehearsals): miss out the high notes (goldfish[11] them), take short rests (explain to your neighbour that you are struggling vocally – you needn't say why), miss out the runs (or, if you are really good, sing key notes but not the ones in between).

The usual restriction during pregnancy is lack of lung capacity; there simply isn't the space for the lungs to expand as they once did. Some pregnant women manage to sing right up to giving birth or within a few weeks of their due date, while others have to drop out much earlier. On starting singing again after childbirth, some women may notice a deepening of their voice, of their timbre, though not necessarily of their range; this is perhaps a sort of maturing. Some may have to

11 Open your mouth without producing sound (a useful technique!).

work hard to get back in the groove. Others sing as they always have. At all events, you should allow enough time for your body to return to normal, and that will also vary from one singer to another and from one pregnancy to another.

Just as there are examples of people who drink like fish and smoke like chimneys all their lives and who don't get liver disease or lung cancer, and also people who have neither habit but contract one or both diseases, it is dangerous to be dogmatic about the effects of age on singing. As we have seen, so many things affect our ability to sing: health (physical, mental, emotional), the amount we sing each week and over the years, how well we sing/have sung, the sort of singing we do, whether we take care of our voices, our energy levels. Singers *may* notice a reduction in range, if anywhere at the top of the voice, possibly a reduction in breath capacity and possibly a lessening of vocal agility. But there are examples of singers who carry on, and have every right to carry on, into their seventies and beyond. One exceptional professional example was the Swiss tenor Hugues Cuénod who continued to sing on stage into his nineties and who died at the age of 108. A remarkable vocal innings and an inspiration to us all. He always maintained that he did not have a beautiful voice, but he sure knew how to use it.

Perhaps more widespread amongst older singers is the *fear* of losing or of having already lost their vocal powers. In my experience it is more often apprehension than reality, more a loss of confidence than a loss of voice, and nothing which some vocal toning won't go a long way to putting right. What may have come naturally once may not be so natural any more, which is why both having and *understanding* a reliable technique are so important. Having a 'natural' voice is great, but, when things go wrong (and they always do), a singer needs to have the know-how to get back on track.

I do see cases of mezzos who have developed a hole between their chest and upper registers. They have lost the transition, the bridge between the two registers. If that area has not been sorted out in the past, it is hard, though certainly not impossible, to repair it later on, but it does require determination and regular guided vocal exercise. You hear this problem in the professional arena too: music-theatre singers who have pushed their chest voice too high for too long and operatic mezzos who have done exactly the same. I would advise being very cautious about taking the chest voice above the F above middle C, certainly on a regular basis… the role of Nancy in *Oliver!* is a well-known vocal graveyard for exactly that reason.

It is worth pointing out that, if you have to undergo an operation that involves a general anaesthetic, you should make sure that the operating team is aware of the fact that you are a singer, so that they take extra care with any tubes that are inserted near or between your vocal chords.

Singers who have had breast cancer and who are prescribed tamoxifen may be warned that it may affect their voice. The medical grounds are unclear, but it is worth raising with your doctor that you are a singer.

One of the most challenging operations for singers is a thyroidectomy, because it involves cutting through musculature which is vital for singing. Singers do recover, but it may take a number of years to re-educate the muscles and re-learn how to sing.

'It ain't over until the fat lady sings' has become a popular throwaway line, said to refer specifically to Wagnerian sopranos, which, sadly, reflects a stereotypical and widespread view of opera singers of both sexes. Do you have to be fat to sing? Short answer: no! Does your weight affect your voice? Short answer: yes! And I am talking about body weight here, not vocal weight (which is something else altogether). Being underweight and being overweight affect the voice just as much as the rest of the body. Ditto putting on weight or losing it suddenly or excessively. Neither is healthy, and singers need to be in good physical shape to sing efficiently. By good physical shape, I mean good *natural* physical shape. Obsessive working out and excessive development of muscles will upset the natural balance of the body required for efficient voice production and should be avoided. Breathing and stamina are the most obvious areas to be affected by variation in weight, but the sound itself may change, too. There is some clinical evidence to suggest that weight loss and weight gain affect men and women differently, owing to the hormonal changes which result. An increase of weight in men may result, paradoxically, in a lightening of their voice, while the same phenomenon in women can produce a deepening, i.e. a lowering, of their range. Is that why tenors are often heavier/bigger than other voices? However, singers who have lost weight dramatically remain uncertain about the precise nature of the relationship between body mass and voice, although there is a consensus view that technique will require adjustment in order to compensate for the physical changes. It is also worth pointing out that, if there is a change in vocal quality, it is usually for the better.

22

The A Word

Auditions! The very word strikes dread into the hearts of most singers, no matter how experienced they are. If anything, auditions are worse for amateurs, because they probably won't have to do very many, whereas for professional singers they are an all-too-familiar, unavoidable part of working life. However, although many choirs do re-audition every three years or so as a matter of policy, a three-year gap is too long for singers to be able to maintain whatever auditioning skills they have acquired.

The common practice in choirs is to ask auditionees to prepare a piece, sing some scales to show their range and do some sight-reading. In addition, some choirs ask singers to sing a set piece and to clap rhythms. An obvious problem is that choir singers do not necessarily sing as soloists, either within the choir or outside, and yet that is precisely what they are asked to do in an audition.

How do you decide what to sing for your own

choice piece? If you have a singing teacher, then you should discuss it with them. If not (or even if you do), you need to ask yourself what the panel is looking for. Usually, they want to hear that you can hold a line on your own, sing in tune and put some expression into your singing. They will also want to assess or re-assess the suitability of your voice for the choir. Please bear in mind that you have absolutely no control over the last criterion. Your voice is either what they want or it's not, and any attempt to make your voice conform artificially to match their ideal is fatal. Don't do it.

Choose a piece with which you are completely comfortable. If a piece has passages or individual notes which you are relying on to be 'all right on the night', don't present it in audition, because they won't be. The auditioning process is nerve-racking enough without any added pressures of that sort. Ditto a piece which you have difficulty in singing accurately from start to finish. The ideal audition piece is relatively short, say, three to four minutes maximum, which shows you off to your best advantage. This is the one part of the test over which you have most control, at least in advance of the audition itself. Sing to your strengths. If you have a completely free rein and are allowed to sing any piece from any period in any language, choose the options which put you in the best light. And don't assume that something you may think of as simple, like a folk tune or a hymn, is easy to sing and won't impress. Simplest is often hardest, because it can show up deficiencies in the best of techniques. I think of the wonderful

Kathleen Ferrier singing *Blow the Wind Southerly*. That simple, beautiful tune requires amazing technical control, which most singers, including professionals, just don't have. Ferrier did have it, though, and the perfectly controlled fragility of her singing that simple air goes right to the heart.

Whatever piece you choose (see Appendix 3 for suggestions), I would advise you strongly to sing it from memory. Why? Because it frees you up to concentrate on the music without having to worry about the copy or the notes inside it. I do realise that some singers find singing from memory very daunting, but I assure you it is worth the effort. But you need to prepare well in advance to make sure that the piece is absolutely secure and so that your memory will not let you down.

Singers are more likely to have trouble with remembering words than notes. Here are a few thoughts on the learning process:

1. When you have worked on the piece to get the notes right and make the words fit the notes, you don't always need to sing in order to practise it or test yourself. You can sit with the score on your lap and go through it in your head, stopping and checking the copy as and when. If you travel to work on public transport, commuting is an ideal opportunity to do this.

2. If you are having trouble with a particular passage, work on that passage in isolation until you get it

right. Then put it in context. It is always tempting to work through the whole thing from beginning to end and never stop to sort out the detail on the way.

3. Singers often devise strategies for learning words. If you keep stumbling over one particular word, see if you can find a pattern in the text to help you. Does it begin with the same letter as a word which comes immediately before it which you can use as a memory trigger? Or is there a word before it which begins with the letter of the alphabet which precedes the letter of the difficult word? Is there an internal rhyme to help you, or a train of thought? Is there something in your personal experience which might link the two words (a bit like devising strategies in order to remember people's names)? It doesn't matter how silly the link is. If it works for you, that's all that matters. You can usually find some hook to hang the word on if you look long and hard enough.

4. Most professionals will recognise the terrifying experience in performance of being unable to remember the word they're about to sing. Their minds go blank. What sometimes happens is that, if they have prepared thoroughly, they will approach the word in a panic, but then hear the right word coming out of their mouth, almost of its own accord and in spite of themselves. The trigger will have worked at a subconscious level, but the preparation

has to have been painstaking and thorough for that automatic memory to kick in.

The best approach to singing the prepared piece in audition is to regard it as a performance. This does take some mental discipline, and the difficulty is that you only learn how to achieve it by actually doing it: the more auditions you do, the easier it becomes, because you learn how you react under pressure and how you can manage the situation in order to do yourself justice.

Which brings us to the subject of nerves. There are two types of nerves: those which take control of you and wreck the performance, and those which cause the adrenaline rush you need for live performance. The first type can be minimised by thorough preparation. Confidence comes from knowing what you are doing and from the knowledge that you *can* do it. If you're going to take the audition really seriously, then sing the piece in front of other people beforehand – as many times as you can. You will learn something new each time.

The bottom line is that you need to allow ample time to 'sing the piece in'; in other words, time for you to become so familiar with the piece technically, emotionally and interpretationally that it is part of you. Only then can you be said to be ready for audition. Here are some thoughts about the day itself:

1. Get there with ten to fifteen minutes to spare: long enough not to feel rushed, but not long enough to start panicking. Be prepared for the auditions to be

running late (quite usual) or early (unusual). Don't let either situation faze you.

2. Wear comfortable clothes, particularly shoes. If this is a re-audition, you can dress more casually than for a first-time audition, but I would suggest that smart(ish) casual is best. You need to feel good in what you wear. Everything helps.

3. Make sure you are warmed up before you arrive, as there may not be a space or an opportunity when you get there.

4. If you can, avoid eating a heavy meal just before the audition.

5. Take a small bottle of water with you, as water may not be available in the venue.

6. Make sure that the copy you give to the accompanist is legible, that the pages turn easily, that the first page is marked with a Post-it (if in a larger volume), and that any markings (especially cuts and repeats) are clear. Loose photocopies, sellotaped pages which are impossible to turn or tatty scores will not endear you to the pianist and run the risk of derailing the whole audition.

7. It is customary for a pianist, possibly the choir's regular accompanist, to play for auditions. If you

want to bring your own accompanist, check in advance that this is OK. It is common practice in the professional world, but has the potential for raising hackles elsewhere.

8. If you intend to sing in another key from the printed one, don't spring transposition on the pianist. Either bring a transposed version of the piece or tell the accompanist in advance what you would like to do and, if they are willing, give them a copy to work from.

9. If you have the luxury of a rehearsal and you need a starting note, arrange with the pianist exactly what they are going to play and practise it with them.

10. Walk into the audition room confidently and in a positive frame of mind. Smile even if you don't feel like it. Practise saying the title of the piece and the composer out loud in advance.

11. If you have a choice of where to stand, stand just in front of the bow of the piano (if a grand) or alongside an upright, facing the panel and so that the pianist can see you. It is quite usual for singers to stand still to collect their thoughts for a moment or two before starting.

12. Have the pulse of the music in your head before you start. Don't just launch in and hope for the best.

13. Indicate when you are going to start by taking a breath which is clear to the accompanist. Take it in time with the music you are about to sing, like an upbeat.

14. If the piano starts the piece, smile and nod at the pianist to show you're ready to start.

15. Don't eyeball the panel, as it will make them feel uncomfortable. There's nothing wrong with looking at them occasionally (though not to judge their reaction), but it's generally best to look slightly over their heads.

16. Avoid standing frozen or rooted to the spot like a statue. You should feel free to move, though not excessively or histrionically.

17. If you do slip up, keep going if possible. If you start wrong-footed, have the courage to stop, apologise (simply, not profusely) and start again. Remember the *Mastermind* technique.

18. Remain 'in the moment' and allow your face to be expressive.

19. Don't forget to thank the pianist at the end.

20. Remember, and accept, that you will not be on top form every time you sing, but that this does not automatically mean that the audition has gone badly.

21. And remember that the panel are rooting for you. They want you to sing well.

22. Singers are usually the worst judges of their own auditions, so don't waste time, energy and brain space dwelling on how it went. Be patient and wait for the letter.

23. There are always things to learn from auditions. Regard them as learning processes and don't beat yourself up about them.

Remember, in an audition, your own choice of piece is the element over which you have the most control. Therefore, it makes sense to focus your attention on that and get it as good as you possibly can. For sight-reading, see Chapter 17, but make sure you leave yourself enough time to prepare. That will almost certainly be longer than you think! Picking up a piece the week before the audition is not an option.

23

Stray Thoughts

1. When the notes go *down*, stay technically/mentally *high*.

2. *Every note has to be painted in.* (Attributed to the wonderful Scottish tenor Joseph Hislop, 1884–1977.)

3. Vowels have a natural volume of their own. EE is said to be a soft vowel, while AH is a strong one. If you sing an AH followed by an EE on a low or medium-range note and you approach the EE with the same volume as the AH, you will overblow or force the EE. To sing a free EE, you have to approach it more as though you are going to sing it more softly. This is an approach only. The actual volume of the EE will be compatible with that of the AH and will not sound out of place. If it does, it's wrong. It may

help to think of the shapes of AH and EE. AH is a rounder shape than the letter-box EE; the volume (think of it in liquid terms) of the AH will swamp the shape of the EE.

4. Similar thinking lies behind what you might call the 'piano probe'. The split second you sound a new vowel or note *is thought of* as piano. This is the opposite of pushing from one note to the other or blasting. It creates the right conditions for a new vowel or note to emerge as it naturally wants to. If there is an audible volume difference between one note and the next, you have got it wrong. It is an approach only. It may be what lies behind the dictum 'All notes begin piano.'

5. When one vowel changes to another, visualise bringing the second vowel over the first one: it comes down over the previous vowel, like a plane coming into land on a runway, where the runway is the previous vowel. This is a variation on Point 1 above. Always think of launching the vowel from side to side, across the column, whether in the mouth or the head. This helps to internalise the sound and keep it within your natural vibrators. This runs counter to 'projecting'.

6. Sometimes it helps to 'will the tension' into your singing. Clearly, that does not mean singing with unduly tensed muscles. What I am talking about here

is natural, correct tension in the vocal mechanism. The vocal chords are in a state of tension when you sing and the tension varies with the pitch. If, for any reason, your chords are too slack for the pitch, it may help to think of an image like a bow and arrow or a rubber band. As the pitch rises, imagine that you are increasing the tension in the bow by pulling the string back as though you are about to fire an arrow. The higher you sing, the greater the pull and the greater the tension. Or imagine that the column is a rubber band. As you sing higher and the column lengthens, so the rubber band lengthens, thins out and increases in tension.

7. As you sing down from the head into the mouth, it may help to think of the vowels creeping along the arc of the hard palate, so that they don't drop straight down to the bottom of the mouth. This is another variation of Point 1 above.

8. Caesari described Gigli as *the great master of flowing liquid tonal beauty*. That's a great aim and an inspiration for all singers. It is the opposite of the 'push and shove' so often heard today and passed off as good singing. Really great singing is physically effortless, because all the body parts are working in complete co-ordination, like a finely tuned engine.

9. Long vowels! Long vowels! Long vowels! It can't be said too often.

10. Once a note has left you, you can't haul it back in if you're not happy with it. It is gone, and you can do nothing about it. Move on to the next note(s) and don't look back. Live in the moment. By all means reflect on it afterwards, but not during the performance.

11. Think of stepping out onto the ice like an ice skater and then not stopping or digging in with the skates once you've started. This is a different way of expressing the column-and-spin principle in order to achieve a true legato.

12. As you sing up the scale and approach the head voice, it may help to think of an hourglass, where the narrow isthmus connecting the two bulbs is where you have to narrow your vision of the vowel. This is sometimes called the *passaggio*, the passageway linking the resonance in the mouth and the resonance in the head.

13. Steps going up the scale are large; steps going down the scale are small. But remember those lift-up points discussed in Chapter 11 and the general narrowing in the riser (think staircase) as you go up.

14. I know of very few singers who are comfortable listening to recordings of their own voice. Many people don't even recognise their own speaking voice, because their idea of what they sound like

is so different from everyone else's. So, if you do record your voice in singing lessons or as part of your practice routine, you need to learn what to listen for. Unless your recording equipment is top of the range, there will be distortion in one way or another. Higher resonances might be cut out; the microphone might be too directional. What you do need to listen for is the resonance rather than the core voice. Don't let it get you down – it sounds much better than you think!

15. Caesari quotes his own teacher, Antonio Cotogni, as saying, *Remember that you must always mentally shape each vowel and impart to it the right colour, timbre, and expression before actually producing it.*[12] That should be the aim of all singers.

12 *The Voice of the Mind.*

Envoi

This book is designed to be an eye-opener or, better, an ear- and mind-opener. Even if it does no more than make you think in a different way about just one aspect of singing, it will have fulfilled its purpose.

Given the title of this book – *Notes for Singers* – it seems appropriate that I should end with a note, or, even more fitting, end *on* a note, a note which might sound like nostalgia. If that means a sadness that we seem to have lost something from the past, then it certainly is nostalgic. But it is not a sadness over the loss of just any old thing from the past, but over the disappearance of a way of singing which I really do believe is the only way which ticks all the boxes.

In recent years, as part of the research for this book and in the course of preparing for students' lessons, I have listened to a lot of YouTube clips of singers and I have found myself growing weary, impatient and frustrated with much, if not most, of what I hear. Fine voices, wonderful artistry, and no real idea how to sing. I find myself in danger of becoming as black-and-white as Caesari himself, and unrepentantly. Listen to the really great singers: sopranos Maria Callas and Renata Tebaldi; tenors Beniamino Gigli, Joseph Hislop, John McCormack and Jussi Björling; baritones Giuseppe De Luca and Carlo Tagliabue; bass Ferruccio Furlanetto. These singers can do anything with their voices, because they know what they're doing. They have the full *messa di voce*, the full range of dynamic, emotional and dramatic possibilities, because they are singing within themselves, from the inside out. Their technique and their interpretation are not superimposed from the outside and, to that extent, grafted on and false. Their artistry grows from within and blossoms at the surface. Nothing is forced – the analogy holds for plants as well as voices. For ease of production and clarity of diction, they cannot be bettered. Theirs is an art which is largely lost. Certainly it is exceptional these days to hear the real thing.

I don't have all the answers; no-one does. Even if I had, they couldn't be compressed into one book or even a dozen. But I hope I have been able to offer a glimpse into that lost art and that I have encouraged you to dig deeper into an activity which is so close to your heart.

Appendix 1

Books by Edgar F. Herbert-Caesari (1884–1969)

No singing teacher has a monopoly of truth, but I believe that Caesari had a clearer, more informed and more consistent idea about singing than the vast majority of teachers before his time or since. If you can get past the grandiose style, the sustained polemic against the 'in-the-mask/forward-production' school (justified, of course!), and the sometimes superseded science, his books are a rich resource, though I won't attempt to disguise the fact that the complexity of the vowel modifications is bewildering when you first encounter it. As I said earlier, his teaching didn't fall into place for me until I had lessons with one of his pupils and could hear the results. But that is no excuse for not reading his books!

Original and early editions are scarce and command

relatively high prices. The London music bookshop Travis & Emery have helpfully republished some of them. In my view, the first two in the list below are the most important.

Science and Sensations of Vocal Tone (J. M. Dent, 1936)
The Voice of the Mind (Robert Hale, 1951)
Tradition and Gigli (Robert Hale, 1958)
The Alchemy of the Voice (Robert Hale, 1965)
Vocal Truth: Some of the Things I Teach. Multum in Parvo (Robert Hale, 1969)

Caesari's last book, published in the year of his death, is a distillation of his lifetime's work, hence the Latin subtitle meaning 'A Lot in a Little'. Though Caesari remained bombastic to the end, the book is an easier read than his other works and you may find it a more accessible introduction to his teaching.

Appendix 2

French Elisions

This is the text of Fauré's setting of *Automne*, a poem by Armand Silvestre, which I have chosen as a good example of elisions (slurs) and hidden vowels in French poetry/song. Letters in bold should be pronounced. An underscore indicates an elision.

Automne_au ciel brumeux, aux_horizons navrants.
*Aux rapid**e**s couchants, aux_auror**e**s pâli**e**s,*
*Je regard**e** couler, comm**e** l'eau du torrent,*
*Tes jours faits de mélancoli**e**.*

*Sur l'ail**e** des regrets mes_esprits_emportés,*
*- Comm**e** s'il se pouvait que notre_âg**e** renaiss**e**!-*
*Parcour**e**(n)t,_en rêvant, les coteaux_enchantés,*
*Où jadi**s** sourit ma jeuness**e**!*

Je sens,_au clair soleil du souvenir vainqueur,

Refleurir_en bouquet les roses déliées,
Et monter_à mes_yeux des larmes, qu'en mon coeur,
Mes vingt_ans_avaient_oubliées!

The elisions in the last line depend on the breathing. If a singer takes a breath after *ans* (as many do), the S would not be elided.

In Verse 3, Line 3, *monter_à* is pronounced 'mont-air à', as mentioned in Chapter 13.

Appendix 3

Audition Pieces

This is a list of easier pieces for those who are stuck for choice. The range of most of the suggestions is deliberately conservative and the pieces are mostly short. If you know you can sing a reliably beautiful top C or a resonant bottom E, then by all means find a piece which has them. Otherwise, play it safe.

For copies, it is always worth checking the free website IMSLP. Many single songs can also be downloaded for very little money.

Voice	**Aria/ Song**	**Work**	**Composer**	**Range**	**Option**
Soprano	*How beautiful are the feet*	Messiah	Handel	F to G	

Voice	Aria/ Song	Work	Composer	Range	Option
	Se tu m'ami		Pergolesi (attribution now discredited)	D to G	Could do A section only
	When he is here	The Sorcerer	Sullivan	D to A	Could do one verse only
	Lascia, mi pianga		Handel	Various keys available	Could do A section only
	The sun whose rays	The Mikado	Sullivan	D to G	
	Spring Sorrow		Ireland	Eb to F	
	Vidit suum dulcem natum	Stabat Mater	Pergolesi	F to Ab	
	Dream Valley		Quilter	Eb to F	

Voices	Aria/ Song	Work	Composer	Range	Option
Mezzo	*But who may abide*	Messiah	Handel	A to E, mainly to D	Can also be sung by a bass or a baritone
	Qual farfaletta amante		Scarlatti	D to Eb	
	Hence, Iris		Handel	Bb to Eb	Could omit B section
	Lascia ch'io pianga		Handel	Various keys available	
	Addio		Mozart	Bb to C	
	He shall feed his flock	Messiah	Handel	C to D	
	Spring is at the door		Quilter	D to F# (optional C#)	
	O rest in the Lord	Elijah	Mendelssohn	C to D	
	Se tu m'ami		Pergolesi (attribution now discredited)	A to E	Could do A section only

Voice	Aria/Song	Work	Composer	Range	Option
	When a merry maiden marries	The Gondoliers	Sullivan	C to F	
Any Voice	*Early One Morning*		Traditional folk song	Key to suit	
Tenor	*But thou didst not leave his soul in Hell*	Messiah	Handel	E to G#	
	Where'er you walk	Semele	Handel	Various keys available	
	Thus when the sun	Samson	Handel	D to G	
	Silent Worship	Ptolemy	Handel (arr. Somervell)	Various keys available	
	Free from his fetters grim	The Yeomen of the Guard	Sullivan	G to G	
	Is life a boon?	The Yeomen of the Guard	Sullivan	F to Ab	
Bass/ Baritone	*Quia fecit mihi magna*	Magnificat	J. S. Bach	A to C#	
	Down by the Salley Gardens	Folksong Arrangement	Britten	Db to Eb	

Voice	Aria/Song	Work	Composer	Range	Option
	The Vagabond	Songs of Travel	Vaughan Williams	A to Eb	
	Sea Fever		Ireland	C to Eb	
	Time was when love and I were well acquainted	The Sorcerer	Sullivan	C# to E	
	Linden Lea		Vaughan Williams	D to E	

Appendix 4

Languages

This section recapitulates and extends the thoughts in Chapters 8 and 13. It does not attempt to be a complete and exhaustive list.

Sung English

Singers do need to be aware of the pitfalls of singing in their own language: it is part of their craft.

The Hidden EE

1. 'Day': a basic example where a Y indicates an EE sound, the second half of the diphthong.

2. 'Endure': there is an implied EE sound here which

singers often miss. Compare with the spoken American pronunciation 'endoo-r', which omits the EE component. The English word should be sung 'en-dee-oo-r', where the EE is thought and sung through, but lightning fast. Other examples: duty, Cupid, execute, use, presume.

3. 'You': the same principle applies: an EE is thought and sung through before the OO, but lightning fast. It does not replace the consonant Y, but enhances it.

4. 'Canyon'; 'Daniel': same principle!

5. 'Queue': 'k-ee-(y)-oo'.

The Hidden OO

1. 'Now': a basic example – 'n-ah-oo'. 'Power' – 'p-ah-oo-ur'.

2. 'When': a W should always be preceded by an OO thought. Like the EE, the thought should be lightning fast. Unless used sparingly for a particular colour or effect, it sounds very mannered to aspirate the H.

3. 'Quarter': 'k-oo-aw-tur'. Applies to any word with QU in it (with the exception of 'queue', as above).

4. ‘Choirs’: ‘koo-ah-ee-urs’.

5. ‘Go’: ‘g-oh-oo’.

The Hidden AW

‘Voice’; ‘rejoice’. AW is an honorary vowel (followed here by IH).

Short A

As in ‘and’. Left unmodified, this is a very ugly vowel to sing on. Think È. So ‘and’ is thought as ‘end’; ‘bad’ as ‘bed’. If the vowel distorts, you have gone too far. It should never sound like 1940s BBC. English is littered with these and they require careful negotiation. Missing one can derail a whole phrase.

Short U

1. ‘Cut’: think (but only *think*) ‘cart’. If the vowel distorts, you have gone too far.

2. ‘Again’: ninety-nine per cent of the time, sing ‘a-gen’, rather than ‘a-gayne’.

AW/O

Many English singers make these vowels too deep, with a pronounced AW which feels like a deep V. To get the vowel to sit on top of the column, think a lighter vowel, perhaps with a mixture of AH in it. Welsh singers do this naturally; so do Italians (though they don't have AW). Once again, it is the thought that counts.

UR

Another honorary vowel. Nothing wrong with singing UR as in 'earth' or 'bird'. Some singers find this difficult, but it is worth the effort.

The Definite Article?

Not as definite as it used to be. As regards 'the', for me the old rule holds good: pronounce as 'thu' before a consonant and as 'thee' before a vowel, so 'thu pear', but 'thee apple'. Sadly, the BBC follows popular usage and refers to 'thu EU'.

Consonants

These are made with lips (labial), tongue, and teeth (dental); of fricatives and sibilants. The hardest ones are H and G, because they impact on the chords. H is aspirated with air across the chords; G is like an explosion at throat level, almost a glottal stop.

The golden rule is that the consonant always goes to where the vowel is. So, if the vowel is in the head, that's where the consonant has to be thought and created. In speech, H and G are formed in the throat (a long way from the head) in ways which, if left to their own devices, will affect the vocal chords. Hence the difficulty.

Experienced choir singers will know that it doesn't take much for an S or a T to machine-gun down the rows if the consonant is not together. Both consonants are easily audible and don't need exaggeration. Even soloists tend to spit out final Ts as though this were the hallmark of good singing (it's not; it's an ugly mannerism unless done for a specific effect), and the same goes for hanging on to a final S like a hiss. It's completely unnecessary.

Exaggerated physical forming of consonants, usually evidenced by a singer's contorted face movements, serves no purpose whatsoever and is usually vocally counterproductive. If you compress your lips to form an M, you clog up the works and you lose the battle before you've uttered the note. The lips should be loose, not tensed, and should meet swiftly and lightly. As the notes rise, so the compression of the lips, which is in any case light to start with, becomes lighter and lighter until the consonant is thought on the head notes and the singer doesn't even think about the lips.

Sung French

French	Memorable Word(s)	Pronunciation Hints	Further Guidelines
–es	*Les,mes, tes, ses, des*	More like 'let', 'met', 'set', 'debt'	Sung more openly
–eur	*Coeur, soeur, fleur, seigneur*	Towards an AH	More open than in speech
O	*La rose*	Approximating to English AW	A darker and more closed sound than in English
U	*Tu, du, vu*	Like the German Ü	Approximating to English 'fuel'
GN	*(Il) ignore*	Like Italian GN and the NY sound as in 'canyon'	
L	*Fusil*	L not pronounced	
L	*Le fil*	More or less like 'feel' in English or *file* in French	
L	*Le fils*	'Feece' (like 'fleece')	
LL	*Bataille, veiller, fille, famille*	LL pronounced as Y; Y sound as in 'canyon'	

French	**Memorable Word(s)**	**Pronunciation Hints**	**Further Guidelines**
LL	*Ville*	Pronounced 'veal' in English or like *vile* in French	An exception
Nasal (M or N) preceded by vowel	*un, bon, parfum, en, enfant;* or as in *intention* (all three Ns are nasal), *embouchure*	Approximates to NG	Usually sung light and fast
Nasal (M or N) followed by vowel	*Mon amour, mon espoir*	A nasal N followed by a short, elided, non-nasal N	Usually sung light and fast
R	*Je ne regrette rien*	An Italian rolled R	Not a guttural French one
Y (vowel/ consonant)	*Payer, pays*	Y as in 'year'	Slightly more pronounced than in spoken French

Sung German

I have tried to find German words which will be familiar to many people as part of their general knowledge.

German	Memorable Word(s)	Pronunciation Hints	Further Guidelines
Short A	*Bach*	The AH is shorter than 'baa'!	Not as long as 'bark' and not as short as 'back'
AH	*Strahl*	AH is longer	
EE	*Beethoven*	Narrower than 'bait'; more towards 'beat'	Closed like French É
EI	*Meistersinger, fein, Wein, Stein, mein, sein, Eis, leitmotiv*	As 'eye' (E plus I = eye)	
ER	*Erde, Erfurt*	Usually pronounced like É	Almost (but not quite) like EE
EU	*Feuer*	OY (approximately as in 'boy' without the Y sound)	
IE	*Wiener (schnitzel)*	As EE (I plus E = EE)	
IER	*Bier*	As in 'bee-ur'	
OE (long Ö)	*Goethe*	Approximates to UR, as in 'hurdle'	OE is sometimes alternative spelling for Ö

German	Memorable Word(s)	Pronunciation Hints	Further Guidelines
O	*Das Gold*	Not as in 'gold', but as in 'doll'	Short, open O
O	*Rot*	Approximates to AW	Long, closed O
B	*Halb, gelb*	Like P when B at end of word	
CH	*Bach*	As in the Scottish 'loch'	
CH	*Ich*	As in the Scottish 'loch'	Sometimes softened to 'ish'
Final G	*Innig*	Like CH (as in 'loch')	
H	*Hannover*	Always pronounce at beginning of word	
H	*Sehen*	Silent within a word	Very occasionally pronounced (for greater clarity?), but safer to treat as silent
QU	*Die Quelle*	Like KF	'Kfelle'

German	Memorable Word(s)	Pronunciation Hints	Further Guidelines
R		Rolled as in Italian	The intensity of the roll varies according to taste and interpretation
S at beginning of word	*Sauerkraut*	As Z	Think of English 'He was despised'
S at end of word	*Das Glas*	As SS	
S within word	*Leise*	As Z	
ß	*Strauß* = *Strauss*	SS	'Sharp'/pure S
SS	*As above*		'Sharp'/pure S
SCH	*Schütz, Schumann, Schubert, (Wiener) Schnitzel*	as SH	
ST	*Strauss, Stockhausen*	As SHT	
SZ	*Bunte Szene* *Die Szene*	S followed by TS 'Buntes tsene' 'Dies tsene'	As though the S is attached to the previous word

German	Memorable Word(s)	Pronunciation Hints	Further Guidelines
TH	*Thränen, Rath*	As T	Outdated spelling still occasionally seen in older editions
TZ	*(Wiener) Schnitzel*	As in TS	
V as F	*Vier ('four')*	Approximates to 'fear'	
W as V	*Wagner, Weber(n), Wolf, Wein*	V	
Y	*Elysium*	As Ü	
Z	*Mozart*	As TS	

Sung Italian

I have tried to find Italian words which will be familiar to many people as part of their general knowledge. These include common musical terms, names of Italian towns and composers, and operas. Foodies will also spot their favourite Italian dishes.

Italian	Memorable Word(s)	Pronunciation Hints	Further Guidelines
O	*Vongole*	The first O is short, the second long long	

Italian	Memorable Word(s)	Pronunciation Hints	Further Guidelines
O	*Troppo, bocca, gnocchi, postale*	Slightly shorter	O followed by two or more consonants
U	*Tutti, Puccini, dubbio*	Puss (in Boots)	Short
U	*Ragu, ritenuto*	OO	Long
Hard C (followed by A, O, U)	(*bel*) *canto*, (Lake) *Como*, *coda, cupola, Cuba*	Like K	
Soft C (followed by E)	*Valpolicella, dolce, accelerando,* *Cesti* (composer)	The E only softens the C; it is never pronounced. As in 'chesty'	I and E soften C and G
Soft C (followed by I)	*Ciao, Montepulciano, arrivederci, porcini, fettuccine, ciabatta*	The I only softens the C; it is never pronounced. 'Ciabatta' is pronounced 'cha-batta'	I and E soften C and G
CH/SCH	*Chianti, l'orchestra, chi, che*	K (like English pronunciation of 'orchestra')	Always hard

Italian	Memorable Word(s)	Pronunciation Hints	Further Guidelines
CCH	*Zucchero*	K	
CU	*Cui*	'Koo-ee', stress on first syllable	A one-off
CU	*Cuor*	'Koo-aw-r', stress on second syllable	
F	*Farfalla*	F not hard like English 'fact', but blown	Loose lips
GU	*Linguine, guardo, guerra, guidare, linguaggio*	'Gwee', 'gwa'' 'lin-gwa-joe'	
GL	*Tagliatelle*	As in 'million'/'canyon'	
GH	*Spaghetti, funghi*	Hard G, as in 'gone'	
GE	*Stringendo, gelati, gelosia*	Soft G as in 'genuflect', or like J in 'jam'	I and E soften C and G
GI	*Don Giovanni, giocoso, giusto, giammai*	Soft G, as in 'jam'. The I softens the G and is never pronounced: 'Don Joe-vanni'.	I and E soften C and G
G	*Ragu, gorgonzola, Pergolesi*	Hard G, as in 'gone'	

Italian	Memorable Word(s)	Pronunciation	Further Guidelines
H	*Ho* ('I have')	O as in 'God'	H always silent
ING	*Stringo, lusinghier*	'Strinn-go', 'loo-sinn-ghee-air'	Never, ever as in English 'string' or 'sing'
QU	*Qui*	'Kwee'	Unlike French
R	*Roma, Rossini*	Roll	At beginning of a word
R	*Amor*	Roll	At end of a word
RR	*Orror* ('horror')	Roll	Double R anywhere
R	*Stringendo, bruschetta, bravo*	Roll	After consonant at beginning of word
R	*Allegro*	Roll	Inside a word, preceded by a consonant
R	*Largo*	Roll	Inside a word, followed by a consonant

Italian	**Memorable Word(s)**	**Pronunciation Hints**	**Further Guidelines**
R	*Morendo, misterioso, calamari, accelerando, tessitura*	No roll	Single R inside a word, followed by a vowel
S	*Giuseppe (Verdi), Risotto*	Like Z – 'Joo-zep-pé'	Followed by a vowel
S(T)	*Antipasto, pasta*	Sharp/pure S	Followed by a consonant
SS	*Bravissimo, assai*	Sharp/pure S	S sounds slightly lengthened when written as double S
SC	*Scarlatti, La Scala, Scorpione, (Renata) Scotto, (mi) scusi*	SK	Hard SC (before A, O, U)
SC	*Prosciutto, pesce*	SH – the I only softens the SC; it is never pronounced	Soft SC (before I, E)
SCH	*Bruschetta, scherzo*	SK (like 'school')	

Italian	Memorable Word(s)	Pronunciation Hints	Further Guidelines
V	*Vivace*	Vibrational, not hard as in English 'vet'	Loose lips
Z	*Donizetti, zuppa, zucchero*	TS	
Z	*Zabaione, zingara*	DZ	Unfortunately we mispronounce the dessert habitually in English
ZZ	*Mezzo*	DS – 'meddzo'	No rule, just learn by rote. Unfortunately we mispronounce this habitually in English.
ZZ	*Pizza*	TS	

Sung Latin

The following words are largely taken from the Latin Mass, *Magnificat*, *Nunc Dimittis* and Fauré's *Requiem*.

Latin	**Memorable Word(s)**	**Pronunciation Hints**	**Further Guidelines**
A	*Osanna*	Like 'and'	Short AH
A	*Sancta, ad, agimus, adoramus, Gloria, agnus, Abrahae, civitatem, facimus, anima mea*	AH (long)	Never short as in 'and'
AU	*Exaudi, gaudete, laudamus*	AH + OO	
E	*Domine Deus, dies, pleni, procedit, Pie Jesu*	É	
E	*Et, ascendit, pacem, perpetua, resurrexit, regni, expecto*	È	You will hear *perpetua* sometimes pronounced as an É

Latin	Memorable Word(s)	Pronunciation Hints	Further Guidelines
ER	*Miserere, erit, perpetua, perducant, semper, ergo, tertia*	'Air'	Different in non-British-speaking countries
EU	*Eheu*	'You' (as in 'pseudo').	Think 'Hugh' with È in front of it.
I	*Sit, hominibus, dimittis*	IH, as in 'sit'	
I	*Miserere, Dei, domine, Gloria, coeli, poenis, civitatem, filius, vitam, venturi saeculi, huic, dimittis*	EE	
O	*Deo, dona, quoniam, nobis, solus, sancto, filio, osanna, hom***o**	OH	No diphthong

Latin	**Memorable Word(s)**	**Pronunciation Hints**	**Further Guidelines**
O	*Domine, tollis, nostram, omnia, hodie, prophetas, h***o***mo*	'God'	
I	*Kyrie, martyres*	EE	
U	*Tuba, venturi, tuam, c***u***jus, Jesu, huic*	OO; (Puss in) Boots	
U	*Solus altissimus, hominibus, lux, cum, cuj***u***s*	Puss (in Boots)	
OE	*Coelestis* (also spelt *caelestis*), *poenis*	AY/É	
AE	*Saecula, aeternam, Abrahae, irae, bonae, caelus*	AY/É	
J	*Jerusalem, cujus* (also spelt *cuius*), *Jesu, ejus* (*eius*), *judicare, judex*	Y	Originally spelt with an I, not a J
C	*Coelestis, caelis*	CH	

Latin	Memorable Word(s)	Pronunciation Hints	Further Guidelines
C(E)	*Pacem*	CH	I and E soften C and G
C(I)	*Crucifixus, facimus, civitatem, benedicimus, ancillae, principio*	CH	I and E soften C and G
C	*Cum, judicare, benedicamus, huic, nunc*	K	Hard when followed by A, O or U
CH	*Chorus*	K	
GE	*Angelorum, genitum, unigenite, generationes*	J	I and E soften C and G
GI	*Virgine, agimus*	J	I and E soften C and G
GA	*Gaudio, gaudete*		Hard when followed by A, O or U
GO; GU	*Ago;* *angustiis*	 'ang-gustiis'	Hard when followed by A, O or U

Latin	**Memorable Word(s)**	**Pronunciation Hints**	**Further Guidelines**
GN	*Agnus, magnam, regni, magnificat*	NY, as in 'canyon'	
H	*Hodie, hostias, haedis, eheu, huic, humiles*	H is aspirated	
H	*Hora*	H not aspirated	
S	*Eleison, homines, martyres, miserere, Osanna, Jesu, exsultavit, misericordia, deposuit potentes, esurientes, divites dimisit inanes*	Z	*Eleison* is a Greek word; I have heard SS (which is probably more accurate). *Dimisit* – usually SS, but I have heard Z.
S	*Jerusalem, prophetas, Deus, saecula, patris, solus sanctus, laudamus, excelsis, Paradisum, finis, Christe, divites dimisit inanes*	SS	

Latin	**Memorable Word(s)**	**Pronunciation Hints**	**Further Guidelines**
SC	*Descendit, suscipe, suscipiant, ascendit*	SH	I and E soften C and G
QU	*Requiem, qui, quem, quoque, filioque*	KW	'K-oo-ee'
TIA/ TIO/TIU	*Gratias, deprecationem, consubstantialem, resurrectionem, orationem, tertia, potentiam, gentium*	'Tsee'	
Z	*Lazaro*	Z	
X	*Lux, exaudi*	KS	

About the Author

Singers and singing have been a lifelong fascination. After spending a dozen years in the choir stalls (Trinity College Cambridge, Winchester and Salisbury Cathedrals) he worked for a decade as a freelance baritone, initially with the BBC Singers and then mainly at Kent Opera, the Royal Opera House and Opera North. He then spent twenty-five years as an agent on the other side of the curtains of the world's opera houses and concert halls. Singing teaching is an ongoing passion. Now in hemidemisemi retirement, he shares his unique experience of the art of singing in Notes for Singers.